AT WORK WITH

THOMAS
EDISON

AT WORK WITH
THOMAS
EDISON

10 Business Lessons from America's
Greatest Innovator

BLAINE McCORMICK

EP

Entrepreneur. Press

Editorial Director: Jere Calmes
Cover and Interior Design: Beth Hansen-Winter
Production: Eliot House Productions
Composition: Beth Hansen-Winter

This publication is designed to provide accurate and authoritative information
in regard to the subject matter covered. It is sold with the understanding that the
publisher is not engaged in rendering legal, accounting, or other professional
services. If legal advice or other expert assistance is required, the services of a
competent professional person should be sought.

Excerpt from the essay "Education and Speed" in the book *The Diary and Sundry
Observations of Thomas Alva Edison* used by permission of the Philosophical Library,
Inc.

Library of Congress Cataloging-in-Publication Data

McCormick, Blaine.
    At work with Thomas Edison : 10 business lessons from America's greatest
innovator / by Blaine McCormick.
        p. cm.
    Includes index.
    ISBN 1-891984-35-7
        1. Technological innovations—Management. 2. Industrial management. 3.
Entrepreneurship. 4. Edison, Thomas A. (Thomas Alva), 1847-1931. I. Title.

HD45.M377 2001
658—dc21
                                                                2001023651

Printed in Canada

09 08 07 06 05 04 03 02 01 ∗ 10 9 8 7 6 5 4 3 2 1

DEDICATION

This book is dedicated to my son, Ellis,
who reminds me—at least 12 times per day—how important it is to stop and
play (see Chapter 10 for why this matters).

TABLE OF CONTENTS

FOREWORD

Help Preserve the Edison Legacy

WE LIVE IN AMAZING TIMES. AMATEURS CREST EVEREST seemingly everyday. Humans are living on the frozen plains of Antarctica. Our spaceships have landed on Mars and even on an asteroid. It seems we've breached our world's final frontiers. Yet at the same time, almost every day, new technologies, drugs, and concepts rearrange our world enough to fundamentally alter what we thought we knew of the world and where we thought we were heading.

It is the talented few, those men and women who are brave, resourceful, and determined enough to challenge conventional wisdom and perceived limits, who are pushing and prodding and sometimes dragging the rest of us through this transformation. And not too remarkably, when asked, many of these pioneers share a common hero: Thomas Alva Edison.

Edison, who gave the world electric light, motion pictures, and recorded music, among so many other transcending technologies, it just so happens, also gave us the blueprint for this time of great and wondrous change. Blaine McCormick's fresh look at our greatest innovator shows us how.

McCormick captures those key pieces that help to define the spirit of Edison: inspiration through perspiration, failure as a fuel for success, forging new paths by throwing out old rules, and applying science to benefit the consumer. He paints a true portrait of the great inventor and at the same time provides invaluable lessons for today's entrepreneurs.

Edison overcame physical disabilities and little formal education to become the most celebrated person of his day. One of the greatest innovators of all time, he has had tremendous influence on modern industrial research and development methods. A team builder, he understood how to organize and inspire groups of skilled individuals to create solutions to seemingly insurmountable problems.

McCormick reminds us of Edison's career as an entrepreneurial risk-taker and owner-operator of a variety of industrial enterprises, in addition to his transcending inventions. What sets Edison apart from his contemporaries and other inventive greats is the balance he maintained between inventing and creating a series of businesses from his inventions—not once, but many times, and in so doing often spawned whole new industries.

Not surprisingly, however, Edison's forte was in creating, not operating or building businesses for the long term. He was more interested in making money from his businesses so that he could continue inventing; he did not invent to make money. He was unparalleled at creating value but less adept at keeping and exploiting it for the future. Finally, he made many forays into many corners of science and had numerous successes. But his never-ending quest for new things also gave rise to some monumental failures. All of this makes Edison not only the father of modern invention, but also the ultimate entrepreneur and the original nerd.

Chapter by chapter, McCormick describes the foundations of Edison's success: finding strength in his own weaknesses; attracting a steady flow of venture capital to feed his enterprises; to being decades ahead of his time in understanding and integrating the concepts of self-promotion and advertising as competitive weapons in his businesses; recognizing the importance of surrounding himself with the most talented employees and colleagues to further his own enterprises; valuing experience above almost all else, and allowing trial and error to help him navigate the unknown when there was no map to consult for guidance.

McCormick also captures the core of the Edison story, a core that is uniquely American, and that makes Edison's trailblazing entrepreneurial career invaluable in educating and inspiring today's and tomorrow's creators: Freedom. Freedom is at the heart of Edison as the great American success story: in giving the consumer more choices and more opportunity, in focusing and structuring a great industrial enterprise so that its ultimate product was *new products*, in the spirit of play and fun, as well as hard work, that must have marked those feverish days and nights when he approached *the* answer to a question, following the thousands of countless hours of experimentation and failure.

Those who are fueling the seemingly endless scientific advances of today owe much to this Wizard of a century ago. They are rediscovering and applying his great lessons: spurring innovation through play (just another word for trial and error) and breaking down constricting structures of conformity, standardization, and efficiency. Who better, indeed, than Edison to look to as a role model, as a metaphor for the value of the scientist and entrepreneur in this great age of technological transformation.

Nowhere does McCormick better capture Edison than in the chapter entitled, "Build Yourself an Invention Factory." Edison had two desks in his Invention Factory, we learn, a rolltop desk where he took care of business (and constantly considered "New Things," as one of its cubbyholes was labeled) and the other was a workbench in the chemistry lab where he invented. It is the interplay and successful union of what these two desks represent, McCormick writes, that enabled Edison to become a legend.

The two desks are of course metaphorical in this story, but it is worth noting that the actual physical desks, preserved the way Edison left them shortly before he died, continue to astound and inspire countless visitors to Edison's Invention Factory in West Orange, New Jersey. Edison earned half of his 1,093 patents here, and also pioneered the concept of team-based research and development. This is where he systematically tackled countless technological quests, sometimes failing, but often brilliantly succeeding. This is where Edison created the invention industry.

Edison's legacy, fortunately, is not only figurative and metaphorical. He left behind for us a treasure trove of documents, diagrams of attempted and unattempted new things, prototypes, some of the world's first films, wax cylinder recordings, early batteries, and phonographs. His Invention Factory is a living legacy, a model classroom providing countless lessons for the future. Yet this key to understanding and appreciating the Edison legacy is in *danger.*

The National Trust for Historic Preservation has listed the Invention Factory and Edison's nearby home, which together comprise the Edison National Historic Site, as one of our most endangered national treasures. The buildings need repair and the collections are deteriorating. We cannot afford to lose this crucial piece of our heritage. The solution is clear: a private-public partnership to ensure that the legacy of the man *Time* named "Man of the Millennium" for his contributions to humanity will continue to inspire genius.

I am President of the Edison Preservation Foundation. Together with the National Parks Service and in collaboration with some of today's great entrepreneurs, we have undertaken an international campaign to raise $80 million to preserve the Edison legacy, including the Invention Factory and its 400,000 artifacts and five million pages of archives, as well as six other Edison historic sites around the nation. As of this writing, we have raised $20 million. We have far to go but are certain we will get there. Edison showed us the way.

Beyond this, we will also celebrate and publicize Edison's ideas, vision, and passion for innovation, stressing his continuing and vital importance to educating and inspiring the young and the not-so-young to explore, tinker, invent and transcend perceived limits. As Edison recognized, there is always another frontier to tackle, another quest to undertake.

Blaine McCormick's worthy book, I am happy to say, captures the spirit and does justice to the legacy of this great inventor, perhaps America's greatest entrepreneur. I hope you enjoy and learn from it. I also hope that the next time you turn on the lights, listen to your favorite CD, or go to the movies, you pause and celebrate, just for a moment, Thomas Edison and his astounding legacy.

Very truly yours,

John P. Keegan
Chairman and President
Edison Preservation Foundation

HELP US PRESERVE THE EDISON LEGACY

Contact:

Edison Preservation Foundation
One Riverfront Plaza, 4th floor
Newark, New Jersey 07102

973-648-0500
973-648-0400

www.edisonpf.org
John P. Keegan
JKeegan@edisonpf.org

PREFACE

AMERICAN HISTORY HAS NOT BEEN KIND TO ITS BUSINESS leaders. In its best moments, history refers to them as "industrial statesmen." In its worst moments, it labels them nothing less than thieves, cheats, and "robber barons." Should an American be deserving of our praise, he or she will be praised for everything but his or her business acumen. President Calvin Coolidge once said, "The business of America is business." American history makes more sense if you put business back into the equation. Behind almost every great American you'll find a great business story. This was true of Benjamin Franklin, the subject of my previous book *Benjamin Franklin's 12 Rules of Management*, and it's also true of Thomas Edison.

He is portrayed by American history primarily as an inventor, but I'd like to introduce you to Thomas Edison the entrepreneur. Edison's legacy has undergone a significant revision during the past two decades as scholars have begun to plow through the millions of documents Edison left behind after his death that are now stored in the archive at the Edison National Historic Site in West Orange, New Jersey. These scholars have discovered and documented an entrepreneurial Edison who was surprisingly talented at attracting capital, promoting new technologies, and managing the process of innovation.

This book was written to take this new understanding of Edison to the broadest possible business audience. In the past, almost every American knew him as "America's Greatest Inventor." In the future, I want every businessperson to know Edison as "America's Greatest Innovator." Inventors are tinkerers. Innovators are entrepreneurs and they, like Edison, can change the world forever.

INTRODUCTION

10 Lessons from America's Greatest Innovator

THOMAS EDISON HAS BEEN DEAD FOR ONLY 70 YEARS, BUT it seems like much longer. That's because so much has changed in the seven decades since his death and a great deal of this change can be traced back to Edison himself. This book was written to help recover his best practices for managing innovation and technology. He is a role model for entrepreneurs struggling to build companies in today's high-tech business world as well as for managers trying to help big, bureaucratic corporations survive in an environment that demands speed, innovation, and "cool" technologies.

By the way, I'm not the only one who has noticed that Edison can be a source of inspiration for emerging business models. In his 1985 book *Innovation and Entrepreneurship*, management guru Peter Drucker called Thomas Edison the archetype for every high-tech entrepreneur. That's high praise from a well-respected management writer. Innovation pays big dividends in today's business environment and Thomas Edison is the high watermark of innovation in American history.

Many of you might be wondering, "So how in the world can Thomas Edison be relevant in today's business environment?" Well, I'll tell you. Whenever Edison introduced a new invention, scores of imitators hit the market, and anybody who could muster a patent claim sued for patent infringement. Music and film pirates illegally duplicated his records and films. Conservatives blasted him in the press for eroding the moral fabric of America when competitors began marketing rather risqué films. As if this were not enough, there were always several small, fast, and ingenious competitors trying to offer improved products just months after he made his initial product introduction. Sound familiar?

You know those big trade shows where the promotional events at each booth compete to see who can be the most outrageous and memorable? We think we invented them but we didn't. A century ago, Edison was staging masterfully directed promotional events when he introduced some of his most important technological innovations, like the incandescent light bulb. "Does Edison have any advice for working with venture capitalists?" the cynics might ask. Yep, sure does. He worked with some of the biggest names in the business including J.P. Morgan and Jay Gould.

Edison's world and our world are remarkably similar. Edison lived and worked in a hyper-competitive, market-driven global economy. His business environment was much more global than most of us realize. In the late 1800s Edison was under intense competitive pressure from a number of European nations. Although most of the international competition was centered across the Atlantic Ocean, it was as vicious as the two-ocean competition we face today. We are just now beginning to recover the global economy that was shattered by World Wars I and II.

THE RISE AND FALL OF CORPORATE AMERICA

Thomas Edison's world and our world are more alike than different, but something strange happened in the decades that separate the two. This strange thing was a period of American history called "Corporate America," and it ruled the country from about 1920 to 1980. Corporate America was a very comfortable place. Life was predictable, loyalty was in fashion, and investors could bank on a steady stream of returns from a set of 30 or so blue-chip stocks. Corporate America reigned supreme and delivered a standard of living that the world had never before seen.

Let's separate American history into three time periods: Pre-Corporate America, Corporate America, and Post-Corporate America. Graphically, it looks like this:

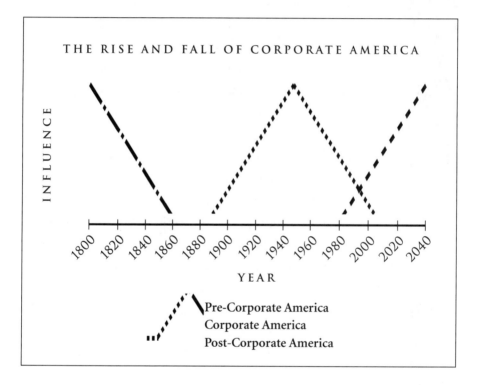

THE RISE AND FALL OF CORPORATE AMERICA

INFLUENCE

1800 1820 1840 1860 1880 1900 1920 1940 1960 1980 2000 2020 2040

YEAR

Pre-Corporate America
Corporate America
Post-Corporate America

Many of us have lived the better part of our lives in the period called Corporate America and can attest to the fact that there are some good things about this period. Big corporations could get things done and created opportunities for Americans all across the globe. Better yet, they were great financial investments. For 60 years we poured our money into "blue-chip" stocks like the "Generals"—General Motors, General Mills, General Dynamics, and

ALFRED SLOAN'S BENCHMARK

Although he never mastered its intricacies, Thomas Edison is believed to have created one of the first multidivisional companies in America. This firm, named Thomas A. Edison, Inc., served to consolidate his numerous business ventures into one complex organization that could be managed by professionals. The pressures of specialization and the necessity of financial controls ultimately killed the innovative spirit of Edison's organizations. However, this was long after he had established his fame with his greatest inventions—the phonograph, the light bulb, and the motion picture.

Alfred Sloan of General Motors is widely credited with creating the first truly successful multidivisional firm when he reorganized General Motors in 1919. However, few people know that before creating his organizational masterpiece, Sloan visited Thomas A. Edison, Inc., for the simple reason that it was one of the only multidivisional firms in existence at the time. Because of visits like this one, Sloan was able to learn from Edison's mistakes and iron out the rough spots of successfully operating a multidivisional company. He later consolidated these lessons in his book *My Years with General Motors,* which became required reading for executives throughout Corporate America.

General Electric—and got some great returns. For almost six decades life seemed predictable and…well…normal.

As good as it may have been, however, it wasn't normal. In fact, it was about as strange as you can get for a capitalist economy. One of the defining characteristics of capitalism is its unpredictability. Up until the time of

Corporate America, capitalism was wild, rugged, and unpredictable. Then for 60 years it was calm, efficient, and predictable. As you now know, we're already returning to wild, rugged, and unpredictable. Corporate America's 60-year reign is only a strange blip when put in historical perspective. It's the equivalent of six straight years of sunny and 72-degree weather in a century of normal, cyclical weather patterns. When put in historical perspective, that's not "the good old days." That's just plain strange.

Edison's inventive nature and business practices emerged in the time before Corporate America. When Edison was getting his start, only a handful of large organizations existed, and these firms sprang from America's first two high-tech businesses: the railroad and the telegraph. The two largest and most important organizations of Edison's early years were the Pennsylvania Railroad (you know, the one from your Monopoly® board) and the Western Union telegraph company. In fact, these two organizations were influential in shaping many of the administrative practices that persist today such as accounting and control practices, regional and divisional offices, and financial reporting.

A few decades later, companies like DuPont, Standard Oil of New Jersey, and General Motors perfected the multidivisional organization and it became the dominant form that subsumed almost all competitors in its path. Along with bigger organizations came more standardization, control, and efficiency. These practices increased both the profits and the market value of the firms adopting the multidivisional organization.

However, new organizational forms proved to be a double-edged sword. Although profits rocketed as firms all over America adopted the multidivisional structure, the quest for efficiency, standardization, and control within these giant new companies gradually squeezed out almost all forms of creativity and individualism. Soon after the coming of the large, multidivisional firm, the dominant image of an American changed from "rugged individualist" to "organizational man." Big organizations dominated the American landscape for about 60 years before they began to unravel under the pressure of international competitors and new technologies like the Internet.

"YOUR ATTENTION PLEASE: YOU ARE NOW LEAVING THE STRANGE PART"

Pre-Corporate America and Corporate America were run by drastically different rules. Corporate America depended on efficiency, standardization, and control. In contrast, Edison's Pre-Corporate America thrived on innovation, individuality, and experimentation. Corporate America loved uniformity and tried to minimize difference—or variation. This mattered on the production line as well as in the human resources office. Edison's Pre-Corporate America benefited from the uniquely talented individuals who were free to walk through the doors of his lab.

Corporate America was also poised to exploit the known. It relied on college-educated professionals who had mastered a body of knowledge and knew how to apply complex theories. Edison's labs in Pre-Corporate America were built to exploit the unknown. Pre-Corporate America had little theory to guide it and learned to rely instead on intuition, experience, and trial-and-error experimentation. Corporate America would have called this wasteful but Edison showed us that it's a legitimate path to success when there are no experts in the unknown.

For the past 20 years or so, America has been transitioning to the stage I call Post-Corporate America. The clearest signal that the good times were over for Corporate America was that size, standardization, and control-oriented management practices stopped being the key to success. During the 1970s, the same American car companies that thrived in Corporate America started to lose market share to German and Japanese imports. More importantly, the 1970s also witnessed the founding and ascent of such revolutionary firms as Microsoft, Apple, Wal-Mart, Federal Express, and MCI to name a few. Although these firms might be considered "dominant organizations" today, then they were operating on revolutionary management and technological ideas—Edisonian ideas. Now in Post-Corporate America, innovation, individuality, and experimentation are once more paying the good dividends.

BIG BAD BUREAUCRACY?

Lest you think that I'm trying to vilify big companies like Ford Motor Company or General Motors, let me state something as clearly as I can: bureaucracy is not the bad guy. Large organizations are frequently the target of a great deal of humor and questionable media coverage. For example, have you heard the joke about "military intelligence" being a contradiction in terms? Or how about those stories that appear from time to time about somebody receiving a letter mailed 40 years earlier through the United States Postal Service?

In all fairness, the USPS has been known to deliver some letters late and put the wrong mail in your box from time to time. However, these occurrences are, by and large, exceptions. Chances are the USPS correctly delivers your mail 95 percent of the time or more. A 95 percent success rate will never make the evening news because it's not considered interesting. In contrast, the 40-year-old undelivered letter is unique enough to make an interesting story. Thus, most Americans get a negative feeling about bureaucracy and other large forms of organization.

We can thank the firms that dominated Corporate America for much of the prosperity we enjoy today. Even though the ideas of efficiency, standardization, and control may not be as popular as they once were, they still pay good dividends when used in the appropriate place. In fact, most of us probably have money invested in some of these "blue-chip" bureaucracies.

TEN LESSONS

Edison lived long enough to see the rise of Corporate America. In fact, many of his most famous inventions actually hastened its coming. A great irony is that Edison helped create the business model that eventually defeated him in the marketplace—but we'll get to that story later. Edison tried hard to fit into the world of Corporate America but he experienced only failure trying to adapt to its rules of size, efficiency, and standardization. He was a transitional figure in every sense of the phrase. He outpaced other businesses in Pre-Corporate America but he could never really keep pace with the businesses that arose during Corporate America. Many of us have already learned that business success in Post-Corporate America cannot be found solely by imitating Corporate America's rules. In the same way, Edison learned that the techniques that helped him succeed in Pre-Corporate America didn't work as well in Corporate America.

I like to refer to Edison as "The Last Great Pre-Corporate American." He is also a great role model for those of us striving to create successful companies in Post-Corporate America. The practices Edison used to find success in Pre-Corporate America are remarkably similar to the techniques that can be used to build a successful company in Post-Corporate America. Mark Twain once noted that history doesn't repeat itself but it sometimes seems to rhyme. Although Post-Corporate America is not an exact copy of Pre-Corporate America, they share some surprising similarities. I've also noticed more and more Post-Corporate America business mavericks consciously or unconsciously using the same tools that made Edison so successful in his day.

I've tried to capture the essence of Edison's business model in ten basic lessons. These lessons are the heart of this book and are explained in depth starting with Chapter 2. Here are the ten lessons with a brief summary of each one.

LESSON 1: *Limit your way to greater creativity.* Edison went deaf during his childhood years and considered this disability to be a key to his great success in life. Chapter 2 discusses the role his deafness played in creating his success and suggests ways that you can limit your way to greater creativity.

LESSON 2: *Talent comes and talent goes, but mediocrity accumulates.* Finding talent was just as important in Edison's day as it is today. Chapter 3 shows that talent played a central role in Edison's labs and suggests a few ways you can attract and retain the best talent.

LESSON 3: *Creativity is all about making connections.* Creativity is a learnable skill and Chapter 4 shows how Edison improved his creativity by increasing the number of connections he made between all the ideas bouncing around in his head. Here, you'll read a poem Edison wrote and learn how it helped him be more creative.

LESSON 4: *If you want to invent, build yourself an invention factory.* Some historians believe Edison's greatest invention was the research laboratory. Edison built two labs he called his "invention factories." If you want to manufacture products, build yourself a manufacturing facility. If you want to invent, build yourself an invention factory. See Chapter 5 for all the details.

LESSON 5: *The greatest innovators have made a lot of Fs.* Edison believed failure was central to the process of innovation and was suspicious of inventions that worked the first time. Chapter 6 reminds us that failure is at the heart of innovation and entrepreneurship.

LESSON 6: *In a capitalist economy, whoever attracts the most capital wins.* Few people know that Edison succeeded as an innovator in large part due to his ability to attract more capital than his competitors. Chapter 7 details this little known side of Edison and also tells the story of how he lost his fortune.

LESSON 7: *The best-promoted technology will often beat the best technology.* Edison's best-known nickname was "The Wizard of Menlo Park" but one writer was observant enough to label him "The Publicity Wizard of Menlo Park." Edison was as brilliant in promoting his new technologies as he was in creating them and Chapter 8 tells how.

LESSON 8: *The price of freedom is a premium most customers are willing to pay.* Edison built freedom into many of his most successful inventions and this chapter argues that freedom is still one of the most important characteristics of any new product or service. Chapter 9 tells the story of the American revolutionary who inspired Edison with his writings about freedom.

LESSON 9: *Play is to innovation what rules are to bureaucracy.* Corporate America lived and died by rules. In contrast, play is at the heart of innovation and Edison banished rules at his Menlo Park lab because he was "…trying to accomplish something." Chapter 10 gives tips to managers trying to revive a culture of play in their workplace.

LESSON 10: *Glow, but don't consume yourself.* One challenge Edison faced in inventing the electric light bulb was finding a filament that could glow with heat but not consume itself in the process. This challenge is a metaphor for Edison's life and the life of any entrepreneur who seeks to follow in the innovator's footsteps. This book closes with a short conclusion focused upon this theme.

WHERE DO WE GO FROM HERE?

This book is divided into three parts. Each part starts with a section called "Interview with an Innovator." These are reprints of actual interviews with Thomas Edison. In his day, Edison was considered our greatest living American and was constantly sought out for interviews. He rarely disappointed the reporters who traveled to his labs and these interviews provide a window into the mind of America's greatest innovator. Following each of these interviews are three or four chapters that build upon its main theme.

Many of these chapters contain a sidebar called "Listen with Your Teeth". This sidebar showcases a variety of Edison's most creative solutions and deliberate strategies for creative thinking. He believed that creativity was a learnable skill and many of his best strategies will be showcased in the "Listen with Your Teeth" sidebars. If you wonder what it means to "listen with your teeth," you'll find the answer in Chapter 2. Also starting with Chapter 2, a section called "E Is for Edison" concludes each chapter by asking you a series of questions that challenge you to make connections between Edison's life and world and today's world.

PART I

INTERVIEW WITH
AN INNOVATOR

"Why Do So Many Men
Never Amount To Anything?"

E DISON WAS ONE OF THE MOST QUOTABLE PEOPLE OF HIS *day. The press flocked to his laboratories to get the latest sound bite and Edison rarely disappointed them. Thankfully, newspaper and magazine archives have preserved many of his best interviews. These remarks are lifted verbatim from an Edison interview published in January 1921 in the now defunct* American Magazine. *His language might be a bit musty by our modern standards. For example, when's the last time you called somebody a "pinhead" or "lunkhead"? Nevertheless, it's pretty clear that a sharp and active mind is producing the remarks. In them, Edison addressed what he believed to be the key productivity problem in every workplace: an unwillingness to think.*

Every man has some forte, something he can do better than he can do anything else. Many men, however, never find the job they are best fitted for. And often this is because they do not think enough. Too many men drift lazily into any job, suited or unsuited for them; and when they don't get along well they blame everybody and everything but themselves.

Grouches are nearly always pinheads, small men who have never made any effort to improve their mental capacity. The brain can be developed just the same as the muscles can be developed, if one will only take the pains to train the mind to think. Why do so many men never amount to anything? Because they don't think!

I am going to have this [sign] put all over the plant:

> *"There is no expedient to which a man will not resort to avoid the real labor of thinking."*
> —Sir Joshua Reynolds

That is true. There is hardly a day that I do not discover how painfully true it is.

What progress individuals could make, and what progress the world would make, if thinking were given proper consideration! It seems to me that not one man in a thousand appreciates what can be accomplished by training the mind to think.

It is because they do not use their thinking powers that so many people have never developed a creditable mentality. The brain that isn't used rusts. The brain that is used responds. The brain is exactly like any other part of the body: it can be strengthened by proper exercise, by proper use. Put your arm in a sling and keep it there for a considerable length of time, and, when you take it out, you find that you can't use it. In the same way, the brain that isn't used suffers atrophy.

Let me cite an illustration from our own organization of how a man can be taught to think; and how, by doing enough hard thinking, he has accomplished something far beyond what would have seemed possible. When I was a youth, I saved the life of a little boy by snatching him off a railway track just as a train was about to run over him. The boy's father was a telegraph operator, and to show his gratitude he taught me telegraphy. Years after, things did not go well with him and he came to see me. He told me that he was down and out, that apparently he was a lunkhead.

He told me he never had invented anything, and he was quite sure he never could. I told him to go ahead and do his best, and that meanwhile I would give him enough salary to keep him and his family alive. By and by he came to me with an idea. We tried it out, but it didn't work. He was discouraged; but I insisted that he keep right at it and see if he couldn't find what was the matter and then try and get around it. He did and finally conceived a workable machine. The concern gladly paid five thousand dollars for it. This so encouraged him that he tried his hand at inventing other things, and became the inventor of quite a number of small things.

By developing your thinking powers you expand the capacity of your brain and attain new abilities. For example, the average person's brain does not observe a thousandth part of what the eye observes. The average brain simply fails to register the things which come before the eye. It is almost incredible how poor our powers of observation—genuine observation—are.

Let me give an illustration: When we first started the incandescent lighting system we had a lamp factory at the bottom of a hill, at Menlo Park. It was a very busy time for us all. Seventy-five of us worked twenty hours every day and slept only four hours—and thrived on it. I fed them all, and I had a man play an organ all the time we were at work. One midnight, while at lunch, a matter came up which caused me to refer to a cherry tree beside the hill leading from the main works to the lamp factory. Nobody seemed to know anything about the location of the cherry tree. This made me conduct a little investigation, and I found that although twenty-seven of these men had used this path every day for six months not one of them had ever noticed the tree.

The eye sees a great many things, but the average brain records very few of them. Indeed, nobody has the slightest conception of how little the brain 'sees' unless it has been highly trained. I remember dropping in to see a man whose duty was to watch the working of a hundred machines on a table. I asked him if everything was all right.

"Yes, everything is all right," he said.

But I had already noticed that two of the machines had stopped. I drew his attention to them, and he was mortified. He confessed that, although his sole duty was to watch and see that every machine was working, he had not noticed that these two had stopped.

Thinking, after a while, becomes the most pleasurable thing in the world. Give me a satchel and a fishing rod, and I could hie [i.e., hide] myself off and keep busy at thinking forever. I don't need anybody to amuse me. It is the same way with my friends John Burroughs, the naturalist, and Henry Ford, who is a natural born mechanic. We can derive the most satisfying kind of joy from thinking and thinking and thinking.

The man who doesn't make up his mind to cultivate the habit of thinking misses the greatest pleasure in life. He not only misses the greatest pleasure, but he cannot make the most of himself. All progress, all success, springs from thinking.

Of course, even the most concentrated thinking cannot solve every new problem that the brain can conceive. It usually takes me from five to seven years to perfect a thing. Some things I have been working on for twenty-five years—and some of them are still unsolved. My average would be about seven years. The incandescent light was the hardest one of all; it took many years not only of concentrated thought but also of world-wide research. The storage battery took eight years. It took even longer to perfect the phonograph.

One great trouble with the world to-day is that people wander from place to place, and are never satisfied with anything. They are shiftless and thoughtless. They revolt at buckling down and doing hard work and hard thinking. They refuse to take the time and the trouble to lay solid foundations. They are too superficial, too flighty, too easily bored. They fail to adopt the right spirit toward their life work, and consequently fail to enjoy the satisfaction and the happiness which come from doing a job, no matter what it is, absolutely in the best way within their power. Failing to find the joy which they should find in accomplishing something, they turn to every imaginable variety of amusement. Instead of learning to drink in joy through their minds, they try to find it, without effort, through their eyes and their ears—and sometimes their stomachs.

It is all because they won't think, won't think!

Chapter 1

AMERICA'S FIRST HIGH-TECH ENTREPRENEUR

A FEW YEARS AGO, *LIFE* MAGAZINE HONORED EDISON BY naming him the "Man of the Millennium," suggesting that his life has shaped our modern world more than any other of the past 1,000 years. To give you some perspective on the compliment, the remainder of the top ten are (in this order) Christopher Columbus, Martin Luther, Galileo Galilei, Leonardo da Vinci, Isaac Newton, Ferdinand Magellan, Louis Pasteur, Charles Darwin, and Thomas Jefferson. Other notables in the *Life* list include William Shakespeare (#11), Albert Einstein (#21), Adam Smith (#74), and Susan B. Anthony (#83). Clearly, Edison heads an impressive list.

Edison was certainly one of America's greatest inventors. When the U.S. Patent and Trademark Office established its National Inventors Hall of Fame in 1973, the first inductee was Thomas Edison. In fact, he was the only inductee that year. The PTO considered his contributions to American culture so singular that all other American inventors—like Eli Whitney, Alexander Graham Bell, and the Wright Brothers—had to wait another year. Edison still holds the record in the PTO for the greatest number of patents—1,093 to be exact. Such facts have long supported his reputation as the greatest inventor in American history. Few people know, however, that he also maintained a record-setting pace as an entrepreneur and businessman.

Edison obtained his first patent in June 1869. Shortly thereafter, he began his first business partnership. During his lifetime he started well over 100 businesses and partnerships. The dual activities of patent application and business incorporation marked his life like twin pillars upholding a continually rising ceiling of achievement. One month shy of his 22nd birthday, Edison formally resigned his job at the Western Union telegraph company and dedicated himself full time to invention and establishing companies to exploit these inventions in the marketplace. America's first high-tech entrepreneur was off and running.

THE ORIGINAL NERD

Self-proclaimed "Silicon Valley gossip columnist" Bob Cringely popularized the term "nerd" to describe the generation of young, unkempt, but technologically sophisticated talent that launched the Third Industrial Revolution in America and heralded the start of the Digital Age. Although he was born a century earlier, Edison was just as much of a nerd in his day as Bill Gates and Steve Jobs are according to Cringely. Edison easily passed the classic nerd tests of shabby appearance, strange sleep cycles, and bad eating habits (pie being a staple of the Edisonian diet).

Interestingly enough, Edison even served as a source of inspiration for the young Steve Jobs, according to Jeffrey Young's book *Steve Jobs: The Journey Is the Reward*. Before he started Apple Computer, Jobs and his friend Dan Kottke took a journey of self-discovery to India to visit the ashram of guru Neem Kairolie Baba. Although the quest had its high points, they also experienced poverty, rejection, fleas, and filth. One day the young Jobs realized, "We weren't going to find a place where we could go for a month to be enlightened. It was one of the first times I started to realize that maybe Thomas Edison did a lot more to improve the world than Karl Marx and Neem Kairolie Baba put together." Shortly after this epiphany, Jobs returned to the United States and the rest is history.

EDISON 101

Edison's life defies tidy summary. It contained too many milestones to summarize in just a few pages. For now, all you need to know is that Edison experienced the equivalent of our modern Information Revolution during his work with the railroads and telegraphs in the latter half of the 1800s. To help get the facts straight, however, here is a listing of the most essential dates in Edison's life.

1847: Born in Milan, Ohio

1859–1862: Sells snacks and newspapers on the Grand Trunk Railroad

1863–1869: Works as an itinerant telegrapher

1869: Receives first patent and enters first partnership

1876: Constructs his own laboratory in Menlo Park, New Jersey

1878: Invents tinfoil phonograph

1879: Invents incandescent light bulb

1882: Installs first complete electrical system in lower Manhattan

1887: Opens new laboratory in West Orange, New Jersey

1891: Invents kinetoscope and kinetograph (forerunner to motion pictures)

1896: Experiments with X rays

1899: Begins experimenting with storage batteries

1907: Suggests that houses can be constructed of poured concrete

1927: Investigates alternative ways of producing rubber

1931: Executes his last patent application and dies later that year

Thomas Alva Edison was born in Milan, Ohio, on February 11, 1847. Not long after his birth, two emergent technologies—the steam-engine railroad and the telegraph—launched what is known as the Second Industrial Revolution in America. Edison became involved with both of these revolutionary technologies by the time he was a teenager. Whereas Gates and Jobs grew up with the microprocessor, Edison grew up with the telegraph.

The family eventually moved to Port Huron, Michigan, and at the age of 12, young Alva—or Al—Edison began working on the Grand Trunk Railroad that passed through his new hometown as it journeyed between Toronto and Detroit. His job consisted of selling snacks and newspapers up and down the aisles of the train. Edison's longevity in the job of railroad newsboy suggests that he had or developed good sales skills during this time. Two years later, his entrepreneurial tendencies became even more evident as he began publishing his own newspaper in the baggage car of the train.

At age 14, Edison's life changed forever when a station agent on the railroad taught him how to operate a telegraph. Telegraphy was the high-tech industry of the late 1800s. A young boy learning telegraphy in Edison's day is roughly equivalent to a teenager learning how to build and program his own computers today. The curious and technologically adept Edison quickly mastered the telegraph and soon began a career as a telegraph operator. Another telegrapher turned American business-legend was Andrew Carnegie. Edison and Carnegie took different paths to business success but the high-tech telegraphy industry gave them an important head start.

Telegraph operators spent their days sending and receiving Morse coded messages across wires that criss-crossed the American continent. In 1860s America, telegraph operators were a society unto themselves and Edison relished both the competitive showmanship and the love of technology that lay at the core of telegraphy culture. Most telegraphers—including Edison—were itinerant telegraphers and followed opportunity from city to city to make their living. For six years, Edison roamed the United States seeking ever more interesting jobs in cities such as Indianapolis, Cincinnati, Memphis, Louisville, New

THANK YOU, UNCLE SAM!

In 1869, Edison received his first patent for an electric vote recorder. This invention allowed members of legislative bodies to record and tally their votes electronically rather than go through the slow process of roll call. Edison fully expected to reap a small fortune by selling machines to every state legislature in the Union as well as both houses of Congress. Much to Edison's dismay, he was firmly rejected by the government on his first sales call to the Massachusetts state legislature.

Not to be daunted, Edison hastened to Washington, DC, under the assumption that he had started too low in the government organization. Surely the federal government would jump at a machine that speeds up the roll call and keeps the minority parties from filibustering to slow the process even more. But what was the federal officials' answer? "Young man, that is just what we do *not* want."

The business-minded Edison had misunderstood the game of politics. Unlike business, politics isn't about speed. In fact, minority party senators would filibuster for days to kill a proposed piece of legislation. An invention that preempted this sacred ritual was despicable. On the way back to Boston, the 22-year-old Edison resolved to never invent anything that did not have what he called "commercial demand." Had Uncle Sam not rejected his first invention, Edison's story might have turned out very differently. As a result of this rejection, he dedicated the remainder of his inventive life to creating value-added products for the marketplace rather than trying to impress politicians.

Orleans, and Boston. Most of these jobs were in Western Union telegraph offices but some were not. The professional culture of the day allowed itinerant telegraphers like Edison to float easily between towns as well as companies. The developmental benefits of such mobility exposed him and other telegraphers to new towns, new personal networks, and—most importantly—new technologies.

The year 1869 was another important year for the 22-year-old Edison. During the previous six years, he had developed a national reputation within the telegraphy community as a first-rate operator as well as somebody who had invented an impressive array of new gadgetry for the telegraph. In February 1869, he placed the following personal ad in the *Telegrapher,* the national magazine for the telegrapher trade: "Mr. T.A. Edison has resigned his situation in the Western Union office, Boston, Massachusetts, and will devote his time to bringing out his inventions."

With this simple announcement, Edison began his storied career creating inventions and companies to produce them. In June of that year, he received his first patent for an electronic vote recorder. By the end of the year he had garnered three more patents for telegraphic inventions. In the fall of 1869, he entered into his first business partnership, a telegraphy-related business called Pope, Edison & Company. The original nerd was on his way and the world would never be the same. Amazingly Edison accomplished all of this despite being deaf, but we'll get to that in the next chapter.

SIX MYTHS ABOUT THOMAS EDISON

Thomas Edison's legacy has reached mythic proportions in America and around the globe and for good reason. Keith Nier, one of several Rutgers University historians working with the archives at the Edison National Historic Site, stated in an interview in the *Atlantic Monthly,* "[Edison] is actually one of the least well known of all famous people, and much of what everybody thinks they know about him is no more reliable than a fairy tale."

ELECTRICAL CONNECTION

Given my previous book, *Ben Franklin's 12 Rules of Management*, you might be wondering if there's some connection between Thomas Edison and Benjamin Franklin. I wondered the same thing as I researched the Franklin book seeking to trace Franklin's impact on American business practice. I expected to find a strong Franklin influence in the life of Thomas Edison. I mean, they both worked with electricity, right? And Franklin did appear as a bust on the family mantle in the film *Young Tom Edison* as well as in a portrait in one of the offices where Edison worked in *Edison, the Man.*

Well, I looked and looked and never came up with a strong historical connection between these two great Americans. Edison did have a favorite founding father, but it was Thomas Paine, not Benjamin Franklin. Edison was attracted to the reason and common sense that pervaded Paine's revolutionary writings. He never looked to Franklin as an electrical pioneer, but then again, the electrical sciences had advanced dramatically in the 100 years between Franklin's kite-and-key experiment and Edison's interest in electricity.

Here's as close as it gets: Edison's authorized biographers, Frank Dyer and Thomas Martin, called him the "Franklin of the 19th Century" in *Edison: His Life and Inventions* which was published in 1910, two decades before Edison's death. Since Edison officially blessed and strongly influenced the content of Dyer and Martin's work, it's safe to say that Edison viewed himself as carrying on Franklin's uniquely American legacy. Not only did he carry on Franklin's legacy, he updated and improved it along the way.

He lived such a large life that it's often difficult to separate the myth (what we believed happened) from the fact (what really happened). In fact, Edison himself was known to propagate some of these myths in order to help the value of the Edison brand grow even larger. His own motion picture inventions further amplified his myth with movies like Mickey Rooney's *Young Tom Edison* and Spencer Tracy's *Edison, The Man*. Let's take a moment to separate fact from fiction in Edison's life.

Edison Myth #1: Thomas Edison invented the light bulb.

Edison Fact #1. Surprisingly, Edison wasn't the first person to develop an electric light bulb. In fact, he is as low as 23rd on one list of people who invented working electric light bulbs. So why does everyone think he invented it? Well, Edison did two important things that his competitors did not. First, Edison invented a better, cheaper light bulb that could be mass produced and mass marketed. In contrast, many of the light bulbs created before Edison's were so bulky and burned so hot that they were impossible to use in the average home. Second, and more importantly, he held better press conferences announcing his discovery. See Chapter 8 for the details of his marketing efforts.

Edison Myth #2: Thomas Edison invented only a light bulb.

Edison Fact #2. Edison didn't just invent a light bulb. Think about it. What good does it do to invent the light bulb when nobody has an electrical wire running to their home? Edison's actual invention was a complete electric lighting system. Growing up with the telegraphy industry helped him understand the importance of inventing a system, not just one product. Telegraphy involved a lot more than Morse code. It was a system of wires, generators, amplifiers, stations, telegraph keys, and operators with their own culture. Edison's ability to think at the system-level gave him an important advantage over his competitors. See Chapter 7 for more on inventing entire systems and the competitive advantage this brings to raising capital.

Edison Myth #3: Thomas Edison was a terrible businessman.

Edison Fact #3. Edison may be one of America's most underrated businessmen and remains unparalleled in his ability to manage the process of technological innovation. In his personal papers, he described himself as having "…the usual inventor's make-up, the bump of practicality as a sort of appendix, the sense of business, [and the] money value of an invention." Edison made three different fortunes and was a millionaire well before he was 40-years-old. (And this was in 1887 when a million dollars could buy more than a four-bedroom, two-and-a-half-bath house in San Jose, California!) His first fortune came from his inventions in electric lighting. His second and third fortunes came from the popularity of his phonographs and motion picture inventions, respectively.

Edison Myth #4: Thomas Edison was a lone genius.

Edison Fact #4. Edison didn't work in solitude but was surrounded by a group of partners and associates that he affectionately referred to as "the boys." He considered invention a collaborative process, one that existed within a deliberately developed culture of innovation. His Menlo Park lab was a rowdy place with no rules, a pet bear, a pipe organ for group sing-alongs, and a revolving door of talent coming and going at all times. You can read more about the work culture at the Menlo Park lab in Chapters 5 and 10.

As for the genius myth, Edison summed it up with his most famous quote: "Genius is 1 percent inspiration and 99 percent perspiration." I believe Edison was a bright fellow (no pun intended). However, I'm cautious to apply the word "genius" to him because it suggests that all of his inventions were effortless products of a gifted mind. He was very intelligent but nowhere near exceptional. I think the difference between Edison and his college-educated contemporaries was that he worked and he worked hard. To call Edison a genius is too easy and allows us to excuse ourselves from mastering the techniques he used to invent the 20th century. See Chapter 6 for more about Edison's trial-and-error process of invention.

Edison Myth #5: Thomas Edison's inventions came to him in a flash of inspiration...you know, like that light bulb above his head.

Edison Fact #5. Edison addressed this myth head-on in a 1911 interview published in *The Century* magazine. The interviewer asked him, "Is it true that inventors are abnormal people, doing their work in a sort of frenzy of illumination?" Edison responded, "Nothing to it. Those long-haired fellows that act strange and figure out strange things, I don't call them real inventors. Once in a while they may hit something, but not often. There are perhaps five hundred real inventors in the world—men with scientific training and imagination. They have made about ninety-five percent of the good things in the way of inventions and improvements. They are usually connected with some big plant; you may not hear of them, but they are there, working out all kinds of machines and processes. They are the real inventors, not the long-haired kind." Of course, by "long-haired fellows" he was referring to our modern conception of the mad scientist with long crazy hair and a white lab coat.

Despite a few "flashes of inspiration," Edison didn't really have a lot of new ideas. Rather he took existing ideas and used them as the raw materials to create "new" ideas. The trail is remarkably clear when you study his life closely. The phonograph wasn't a new idea but a logical extension of his inventions in the field of telegraphy. His system of electricity was remarkably similar to the gas lighting systems that were already in place. Many of his inventions have strangely familiar parallels to the telegraph industry. What we now call "inspiration" was really just applying a strong base of personal experience to a variety of new challenges. See Chapter 4 for more about how a broad base of personal experiences can foster more creativity.

Edison Myth #6: As a child, Thomas Edison saved his mother's life by inventing a makeshift but well-lit operating room using an ingenious mix of kerosene lamps and mirrors so the family doctor could perform a lifesaving operation at night.

Edison Fact #6. No, that's just the movies. In 1940, MGM released *Young Tom Edison* with Mickey Rooney and *Edison, the Man* with Spencer Tracy. Although both films made a well-intentioned effort to honor Edison's memory, they ended up showing more myth than reality. Mickey Rooney may have stopped a doomed steam train by sending a Morse code message to his sister with a steam whistle but Edison never did. Spencer Tracy started out as a penniless, family-loving janitor but that was never Edison. The real Edison story is much more fascinating than anything to come out of Hollywood. And remember, it was not *Young Tom Edison*, it was young Alva Edison.

Chapter 2

TURNING A DEAF EAR (INTO A COMPETITIVE ADVANTAGE)

WHY IS THIS MAN SMILING? TURN THE PAGE FOR THE ANSWER.

(Photo courtesy of U.S. Department of the Interior, National Park Service, Edison National Historic Site)

THE ANSWER: *Thomas Edison was deaf but knew that this deafness was a key source of his success. This photo was taken toward the end of his life after he had taken plenty of time to reflect on the role of this alleged "disability." I suspect he knew his deafness had brought him more happiness and success than sorrow.*

SO, WHAT HAPPENED?

HARVARD BUSINESS SCHOOL PROFESSOR MICHAEL PORTER ARGUES that strategy is all about being different. Some of us are born different. Others achieve difference. Still others have difference thrust upon them. Thomas Edison was different and this difference was thrust upon him when he was a young man.

In an interview given many years after the incident, he described the accident that resulted in his deafness like this:

> *I became deaf when I was about twelve years old. I had just got a job as newsboy on the Grand Trunk Railway, and it is supposed that the injury which permanently deafened me was caused by my being lifted by the ears from where I stood upon the ground into the baggage car. Earache came first, then a little deafness, and this deafness increased until at the theater I could hear only a few words now and then. Plays and most other 'entertainments' in consequence became a bore to me, although I could imagine enough to fill in the gaps my hearing left. I am inclined to think I did not miss much. After the earache finally stopped I settled down into steady deafness.*

The exact cause of Edison's deafness remains unknown despite this autobiographical statement. Surprisingly, he gave conflicting stories about how he became deaf. Later in his life, he embellished the story about being lifted into the boxcar by adding that he "felt something snap" inside his head. Another time, he claimed that a baggage master on the railroad "got a bad burn and boxed my ears severely" after the curious Edison accidentally started a chemical fire in the baggage car while experimenting with some chemicals.

Despite these and other conflicting tales of disease and fevers, it's clear that Edison noticed something had gone very wrong with his hearing a few years into his teenage life. Whatever it was, it ultimately progressed to a stage of almost complete deafness. Edison was left with a little hearing in his right ear and could carry on a conversation with anybody willing to speak loudly into that ear.

He made some remarkable (and downright inspirational) statements about his deafness as he got older. In another interview he stated , "I have been deaf ever since [these childhood incidents] and the fact that I am getting deafer constantly, they tell me, doesn't bother me. I have been deaf enough for many years to know the worst, and my deafness has been not a handicap but a help to me." This is an extraordinary statement.

In the business world, when we think of "helpful" we think of "competitive advantage." Later I'll discuss some of the specific benefits Edison received from his deafness. First, however, I want to spend a little time clarifying this idea of competitive advantage.

CALL THE SWOT TEAM!

One of the first great analytical tools for formulating strategy was the SWOT analysis. SWOT stands for Strengths, Weaknesses, Opportunities, and Threats and a SWOT analysis focuses on understanding a company's internal strengths and weaknesses and the external opportunities and threats that exist in the company's business environment. SWOT analysis is a tool to help you find the best fit possible between your *internal* strengths and weaknesses and *external* opportunities and threats. Once they are identified, you are supposed to capitalize on strengths, build defenses for weaknesses, capitalize on opportunities, and avoid threats whenever possible.

LUV IS DEAF, TOO

Southwest Airlines is nobody's idea of a normal company. Absurdities abound at the Dallas-based carrier. For example, their stock ticker symbol—LUV—is derived from the name of the airfield in Dallas where they got their start in the late 1960s. However, their start was anything but easy. Early in their history, established airlines used existing airline regulations to argue that Texas did not need another airline and Southwest had to engage in a lengthy legal battle just to stay in the air.

Later, opposing interests saddled Southwest with what appeared to be a severely restrictive limitation: the Wright Amendment. This federal law forced all traffic flying out of Dallas's Love Field to have a final destination in either Texas or one of its four neighboring states—Louisiana, Arkansas, Oklahoma, or New Mexico. This meant that any airline operating out of Love Field would be limited to short-haul flights—foregoing the seemingly more lucrative long-haul, interstate routes.

Shortly after deregulation of the airline industry and passage of the Wright Amendment, Southwest's management team met to decide the future of the company. Surprisingly, they chose to stay committed to the low-cost, short-haul strategy that they had been forced into by opposing interests. Since that time, Southwest Airlines' CEO, Herb Kelleher, has proceeded to build one of the most successful airlines in the industry around a short-haul, quick-turnaround strategy that has paid incredible dividends for almost 30 years. Southwest's choice to limit itself to a specific market niche has made them the only airline to post a profit every quarter since 1973.

Let's focus on that "W"—weaknesses. The common wisdom is to be aware of your weaknesses in order to protect yourself from attack in those areas. Edison's life turns this common wisdom on its head and suggests that your weakness may be the best place to start building your competitive advantage. In other words, your weakness may not be a *real* weakness but just a *perceived* weakness. The good news is that your perceived weaknesses may be a competitive advantage waiting to happen.

So what do we mean by competitive advantage? There's a lot of talk in strategic management circles about this concept of competitive advantage. In fact, the phrase occurs in a surprising number of business titles, starting with Harvard Business School professor Michael Porter's seminal 1985 strategy text, *Competitive Advantage*. The idea must have caught on because even the most casual review of recent business books uncovers such titles as *Competitive Advantage Through People, Benchmarking for Competitive Advantage,* and *Data Mining: Building Competitive Advantage*. Competitive advantage seems to be a bandwagon onto which everybody wants to hop. However, too many of us may find ourselves waving the words around like a magic wand hoping that they might change something when we really have very little understanding of what the phrase actually describes. Let's try to clear up some of this thinking.

Try to think about the concept in terms of three possible business results: competitive disadvantage, competitive equality, and competitive advantage. Competitive disadvantage may sound impossible but it happens more often than you might think. Edison believed that some disadvantages were worse than deafness. For example, in his personal papers he wrote, "While I was a newsboy on the Grand Trunk I had a chance to learn that money can be made out of a little careful thought, and, being poor, I already knew that money is a valuable thing. Boys who don't know that are under a disadvantage greater than deafness."

Competitive disadvantage can occur when managers misunderstand the role and value of money. It also occurs when a business doesn't have the resources necessary to keep up with existing or new competitors. When a company runs out of cash or working capital, or fails to update technologically, or when a new competitor ups the stakes of the game, they may find themselves working at a competitive disadvantage. Obviously, businesses that operate at a competitive disadvantage cannot survive for long.

Competitive equality means you're a little better off but it's still not the best of all possible worlds. Lots of businesses operate in a state of competitive equality because our particular brand of American capitalism is designed to promote this ideal. Competitive equality means you're not at a competitive disadvantage, but neither are you at an advantage over any of your competitors. You can meet payroll, keep a healthy cash flow, repay your stakeholders, and make enough profit to plow some of it back into your firm for the next year. Competitive equality means you'll always make it another year but will never get a special edge over any of your competitors.

Competitive advantage is about having that special edge. More than that, it's an edge that your competitors do not have, one that helps you earn more profit than the average company in your peer group. In addition, competitive advantage usually means that whatever you have can't easily be imitated by your competitors. Let me try to illustrate this concept. It may be having a particular location that nobody else has, especially when this locational advantage can't be duplicated as in the case of waterfront property. Competitive advantage may mean that you have a unique company culture that nobody else has. Can your competitors go out and buy themselves a unique culture? No! It may also mean that you have some proprietary technology or brand equity or maybe even a unique collection of talented people in your organization.

Now for the strange twist: Deafness was Edison's competitive advantage. His "handicap" gave him an advantage that nobody else could imitate. Best of all, it was an advantage that nobody would ever want to imitate. Can you imagine a company president volunteering to lose his hearing so he can better understand Edison's way of thinking? It's never going to happen! *Ergo*, competitive advantage.

HEY, HILLBILLY!

Thirty years ago, nobody thought to look in rural America for the next great business opportunity. In fact, nobody thought to look to rural America for anything other than a few good jokes about the population. Sitcoms like *The Beverly Hillbillies* summed up what most people thought existed in America's mountainous, non-urban regions, like Arkansas or West Virginia. That was before Sam Walton came along.

Walton transformed a small chain of discount retailers in small towns throughout rural Arkansas into the nationally known retailer Wal-Mart. Prior to Walton, no businessperson considered rural America as a place to find a competitive advantage. In fact, anything rural usually ended up in the "Weakness" category in the SWOT analysis. However, nobody seemed to tell Sam Walton this fact. Before long, he had pieced together a system of stores throughout rural America and became the dominant retailer in each small town where he operated.

Ultimately, other discount retailers realized the goldmine Walton had found. It was too late, however. Building from a traditional weakness, he established a system that successfully resisted new entrants from competitors. This system of high-performing stores also proved to be a prosperity engine that funded Walton's expansion into urban markets where he successfully took market share away from competitors who had no equivalent prosperity engine to fund their operations. Sometimes competitive advantage is found in the most unlikely places.

Strategy consultants counsel that you should build your competitive position around well-protected market niches that defy invasion from competitors. Most companies look to their list of strengths to seek out their competitive advantage. Edison's life suggests that we ought to be looking in the weakness column of the SWOT analysis to find our competitive advantage. Building a competitive advantage around a weakness—like loss of hearing—is doubly beneficial since nobody would ever think of taking on that weakness in order to overtake you in the marketplace. Furthermore, it's just not common wisdom to look at weaknesses as sources of competitive advantage. For the unconvinced, let's take a closer look at how Edison's weakness gave him some great personal benefits and ultimately led to a unique competitive advantage that nobody else could imitate.

THREE GOOD THINGS ABOUT BEING DEAF

Edison got quite specific about how his deafness helped him throughout his life. Among other things, he believed it helped him become a better reader, gain a better focus, and be more creative.

Gaining an educational advantage. Throughout history, great businesspeople have been strong readers. This has been true of managers, from Benjamin Franklin to Bill Gates. Edison was no exception and attributed his love of reading to his deafness. He made the following comments in some autobiographical reflections: "From the very start, after the pain ceased, deafness probably drove me to reading. My refuge was the Detroit Public Library. I started, it now seems to me, with the first book on the bottom shelf and went through the lot, one by one. I didn't read a few books. I read the library. Then I got a collection called *The Penny Library Encyclopedia* which was published in Dublin, and read that through."

It's quite possible that Edison overstated himself a bit when he claimed to have read the entire Detroit Public Library—although it's likely that public

GOOD NEWS FOR THE VISUALLY CHALLENGED

Sir William Petty was a 17th-century political economist who, among other things, developed the balance-of-trade concept and coauthored the first book on statistics. He was also clever enough to turn his primary weakness—nearsightedness—to his advantage in life-threatening situations. In 17th-century England, nothing could be more life threatening to an intellectual than to be challenged to a duel.

Despite its seemingly barbarian nature, conflict resolution by dueling had strict rules of protocol designed to even the playing field between the two adversaries. This protocol held that when a challenger initiated a duel, the individual challenged was given the choice of weapon and location (such as "Guns at high noon on Main Street!"). This self-policing rule supposedly allowed the challenged to play to their strengths. Not so with Sir William. He played to his weakness. On one occasion when he was challenged to a duel he responded, "Axes, in a dark cellar," thereby eliminating any advantage his opponent might have enjoyed in terms of better vision or marksmanship. Needless to say, the other fellow withdrew.

libraries were considerably smaller then than they are now. Nonetheless, it's clear that he consumed a great deal of material at an early age, primarily because this was the only form of entertainment available for an individual with hearing problems. As his reading progressed, Edison learned to tackle bigger and bigger texts that ultimately served as his formal education. He notes, "I read Burton's *Anatomy of Melancholy*—pretty heavy reading for a youngster. It might have been, if I hadn't been taught by my deafness that almost any book will supply entertainment or instruction. By the time I tackled *The Anatomy of Melancholy* I could enjoy any good literature, and had found that there was virtually no enjoyment in trash. Following the *Anatomy* came Newton's *Principles.*"

Edison didn't limit his reading to the science or reference shelf but regularly indulged in all kinds of literature. We do know that the French romantic Victor Hugo was one of Edison's favorite authors and that he particularly enjoyed Hugo's novel *The Toilers of the Sea*. As a child, Edison was intrigued by the pulp adventure and spy novels of Sylvanus Cobb, Jr. like *The Gun Maker of Moscow*. However, the anchor of Edison's bookshelf was probably Thomas Paine's *The Age of Reason,* of which I'll have more to say in Chapter 9.

In sum, Edison's deafness most likely resulted in an advantage as a result of his massive self-education efforts due to a lack of other, more entertaining options. It's also clear that he learned to tell the difference between value-added reading and reading that he termed "trash. " The more you read, the more likely you are to know a high-impact book when you see it, and Edison returned to such books again and again.

Gaining a focus advantage. Do you ever struggle with keeping your attention focused on the task at hand? This is especially difficult when the task at hand is complex and there's a variety of interesting options only a few clicks away on the Internet. Edison found that his deafness insulated him from distraction, both on the job and on the street.

In one of his autobiographical reflections, he writes about the advantages of being deaf in the telegraphy business: "From the start I found that deafness was an advantage to a telegrapher. While I could hear unerringly the loud ticking of the instrument, I could not hear the instruments of the man next to me in the big office. I became rather well known as a fast operator, especially at receiving." To better appreciate this comment, you must understand a bit about how work was arranged in big telegraph offices. Midsize offices, like some of the ones where Edison worked, could consist of up to a dozen operators working at transmitters in the same room. Headphones had not yet been invented, so the room could be filled with the noise of a dozen incoming telegraphs at the same time.

Can you imagine how difficult it might be to stay focused on your incoming telegraph and disregard others during a peak period? It's easy to see how a limited range of hearing could improve your receiving speed when you didn't have to filter out the other incoming messages. There's a legendary story about weeding out applicants in the telegraph industry. As it goes, job applicants would be asked to report to a waiting room located near where the telegraph operators were receiving their messages. In addition to the regular noise of incoming messages, an automatic telegraph would be repeating, "If you can hear this message, please go immediately through the door into the next room. You're hired!" Only a handful of the most focused applicants would pick up the message, but in doing so they would prove their ability to focus on the task at hand and ignore all other distractions.

Edison found freedom from distraction liberating off the job as well. He noted in his personal reflections that, "It may be said that I was shut off from that particular kind of social intercourse which is small talk. I am glad of it. I couldn't hear, for instance, the conversation at the dinner tables of the boardinghouses and hotels where, after I became a telegrapher, I took my meals. Freedom from such talk gave me an opportunity to think out my problems."

In our modern information-driven economy where networking pays big dividends, we might think that Edison was at a disadvantage even though he stated otherwise. Let's face it, he might have picked up some valuable ideas from dinner conversations at the next table or the person walking next to him on the street. That might be true today, but Edison's times were different. Chances are the people sitting next to him in a boardinghouse couldn't come close to helping him work out the glitches on whatever invention was fermenting in his rich mind. His freedom from such petty annoyances most likely resulted in him having a competitive advantage when it came to staying dedicated to the task at hand.

LISTEN WITH YOUR TEETH
How (and Why) to Listen with Your Teeth

Throughout his life Edison had to find a way to compensate for his lack of hearing, especially when he was involved with such inventions as the phonograph or when he needed to listen closely to messages coming through the telegraph. One favorite solution was to use his teeth to transfer the sound vibrations to his jawbone so he could better differentiate among the various frequencies of sound.

With the phonograph, he simply bit down on the edge of the speaker horns that amplified the sounds coming from the original phonographs. Prior to the phonograph, Edison worked on an invention he called "the speaking telegraph" that was roughly equivalent to the telephone. In order to test the acoustic properties of various configurations of the invention, Edison created a metal plate attached to the sounding apparatus of the telegraph. He could then hold this plate in his teeth to transfer the sound vibrations to his resonating jawbone. Although such stories might make fingers curl on readers with sensitive teeth, you have to admit that Edison's creative solutions merit admiration.

So what does this have to do with helping you be more creative? Well, try approaching your current problem from the perspective of a disabled person. Ask yourself, "How can a deaf person hear Morse code?" or "How can a blind person drive?" Assuming a disability when problem solving might give you the inspiration to approach your current problem from important new perspectives. Like Thomas Edison, you may find that putting limitations on yourself will spur you to even greater creativity.

Gaining a creative advantage. Edison also attributed much of his creative success to his deafness. In fact, he stated in no uncertain terms that his first great invention, the phonograph, came about as a result of his deafness. It makes sense, doesn't it? He also claimed to have contributed to the more rapid development of the invention of the telephone by Alexander Graham Bell. He argued in his personal papers that, "Deafness has done many good things for the world. In my own case it has been responsible, I think, for the perfection of the phonograph; and it had something to do with the development of the telephone into usable form. When Bell first worked out his telephone idea I tried it and the sound which came in through the instrument was so weak I couldn't hear it. I started to develop it and kept on until the sounds were audible to me. I sold my improvement, the carbon transmitter, to the Western Union and they sold it to Bell. The telephone as we now know it might have been delayed if a deaf electrician had not undertaken the job of making it a practical thing."

Edison also claimed that his deafness helped him problem solve as well as invent. One story tells how he was called to New York City to help solve noise problems associated with the new elevated trains in that city. A number of people had tried to find ways to make the elevated trains less noisy but could never seem to pinpoint the precise location of the noise. Due to his deafness, Edison could only hear the worst of the noise. This allowed him to more quickly pinpoint the problem area, whereas other experts had been distracted and sidetracked by other noises made by the elevated trains. It turned out that the noise was due to structural problems with the elevated tracks and not the steam engines that ran the train. While most observers couldn't hear past the engine, Edison could hear the heart of the problem due to his "disadvantage."

LIMIT YOUR WAY TO SUCCESS

I tend to think of weaknesses and limitations the same way. Nobody wants to admit they have weaknesses and nobody wants to put any kind of limitations on themselves. As a result, limitations and weaknesses are the last places most people would look for competitive advantage—so they may be the best places to create it. Late in his life, when medicine had advanced beyond what it was in his younger years, Edison claimed that a hearing specialist approached him and offered to help restore part or all of his hearing. He turned down the offer, however, and preferred to remain deaf due to the great benefits he had received from his severe hearing limitations. Edison had learned that limitations were an essential part of his creativity. It's a concept that still applies today.

Consider the case of the vanity license plate. I lived in California for two years and learned that the vanity plate is a form of creative expression in the Golden State. The limitations on this art form are staggering: seven available spaces (less in some states), and 26 letters of the alphabet, ten numbers, and a handful of symbols like stars or hearts to choose from.

Despite—or rather because of—these limitations, creativity has flourished on vanity plates. See if you can figure out a few of the following examples (answers are in the sidebar on page 48):

2L82W8

MONEPIT

MTBRAIN

QT PI

XQUS ME

GU10TAG

S5280FT

RECHDXS

2N2R4

The Children's Television Workshop, creators of the long-running children's program *Sesame Street* are pioneers in the area of visual education. *Sesame Street* is also a perfect example of how limits actually foster creativity. *Sesame Street's* programming content for over 30 years has been the 26 letters of the English alphabet and the numbers one to nine. Couple that with a target audience of preschool children and a network that relies on public

TOO CHICKEN TO TRY 24/7?

The numbers "24/7" have come to symbolize our current pace of work in America. Should you somehow have evaded the meaning of this phrase, it means that you work or will work "24 hours a day, 7 days a week" on whatever task you sanctify with the phrase. As hectic as that might sound, there's a firm out there that has consciously chosen to adopt a 24/6 stance. That is, this firm will dedicate itself to accomplishing its objectives 24 hours a day, 6 days a week. Put differently, same competitive pace but one less day of work…by choice. The company is Chick-fil-A and the policy is unique in the restaurant industry.

During the years following World War II, Truett Cathy experimented in his small diner with a variety of ways to fry chicken. He ultimately perfected a one-of-a-kind chicken sandwich served on a toasted buttered bun with two pickle chips. In 1967, Cathy took this sandwich and opened a restaurant in a shopping mall in Atlanta. It was the beginning of the in-mall, quick-service food industry. His firm has since expanded beyond shopping malls into stand-alone outlets and cafeterias on college campuses. His competitors have imitated him at every turn with one exception: Chick-fil-A closes on Sunday.

Closing on Sunday might be considered suicidal in the restaurant industry. Nevertheless, Chick-fil-A has been doing it for decades and has grown. The decision to close on Sunday is a self-imposed limit that focuses activities closely on how to best leverage the other six days of the week. With no "big weekend" to save them, Chick-fil-A has had to think creatively about how to best their competitors with one seventh less time. It's a perfect example of how limits can force you to be even more creative.

donations for survival, and they're dealing with some serious limitations. Yet *Sesame Street* has managed to make this otherwise dull, limited content come to life in a thousand and one different ways.

"A" is not just a letter, but becomes an airplane and an apple and an aardvark. A variety of clever songs, animation, and some of Jim Henson's greatest muppet creations work to keep the focus on the core content: the alphabet and numbers. In a 1926 interview in *The Forum* Edison stated, "It is impossible to fascinate young minds with dull complexities." *Sesame Street* exemplifies Edison's vision of making education visually interesting work as opposed to textually dull work.

American jazz icon Wynton Marsalis also heralds the virtues of limitations when it comes to creating great jazz. I once heard a radio interview in which Marsalis stated that great jazz is created only when musicians choose to limit themselves to certain scales or rhythms or notes. A jazz novice like me might easily assume that a complete absence of boundaries would be the ideal environment to foster a free-form, spontaneous, creative musical form like jazz. However, Marsalis's comment suggests I'm dead wrong. The best jazz can only be created in the presence of socially agreed upon limitations. With-

2L82W8—too late to wait

MONEPIT—money pit

MTBRAIN—empty brain

QT PI—cutie pie

XQUS ME—excuse me

GU10TAG—gutentag ("good day" in German)

S5280FT—smile (a mile is 5,280 feet...get it?)

RECHDXS—wretched excess

2N2R4—two and two are four (probably a school teacher)

out such limitations, claims Marsalis, jazz falters. He summed it up in the radio interview when he described trying to create without the benefits of self-imposed limits: "That's not inspiration, that's desperation."

From a business standpoint, "desperation, not inspiration" sums up the basic strategy of many conglomerates. The conglomerate was perfected in the 1960s with firms like Litton Industries, Textron, ITT, and LTV serving as its poster children. The basic idea behind conglomerates was to get into as many unrelated (yes, unrelated) businesses as possible in order to spread around the risk of operating in cyclical industries.

Conglomerate managers hoped that most of their businesses would be up when some of their industries were down. In fact, the herd instinct seemed to be that the more businesses you had, the more likely you were to have a majority of them on the upswing. Therefore, managers acquired a wide array of increasingly unrelated businesses. One conglomerate (I swear I'm not making this up!) oversaw businesses in auto parts, cement, cigars, apparel, video games, horse racing, and sugar. Such managers hoped that growth through acquisition would result in ever-increasing profits and a skyrocketing stock price.

This "desperation" strategy seemed to work for a while but the house of cards came crashing down in the late 1960s. Since that time, most conglomerates have ceased to exist and those that remain pursue a deliberate strategy of only acquiring companies that are in some way related to their existing businesses. Much of the latest thinking in strategic management suggests that a focused, related strategy is the best way to ensure long-term profitability. Current strategy gurus suggest building your strategy around a set of limitations known as your core competencies.

Core competencies are activities and processes that your firm does better than anybody else. For example, one of Disney's core competencies is animation. Their animated films regularly make $100 million and more in the United States alone. Furthermore, Disney has proven to be an innovator in this area with computer-generated animation films like *Toy Story* and *Dinosaur*. Although it might seem like a limitation at first blush, Disney has built a remarkably large business empire by letting their animation activities create new directions for their theme parks, live action shows, and retail stores. In the end, the inspiration that comes from limiting or focusing your activities probably pays better dividends than the desperation of leaving all your options open.

ADVICE FOR YOUR NEXT INTERVIEW

One of the worst questions you can ask someone during a job interview is, "What is your greatest weakness?" Yet this question continues to be a perennial favorite on lists like "Ten Knockout Interview Questions That Get Results!"—and usually appears just after the one about the candidate's greatest strength. What are we expecting here, folks? Nobody's going to open up during a job interview and state, "Well, quite honestly, my greatest weakness is that I just can't resist shopping online after I return from my two-hour lunch break."

Anyone who has interviewed for more than one job during their career has probably been asked this question and figured out that there are two great stock answers: "I'm a perfectionist," or "I continually find that I take on too much responsibility." Each of these responses can be effective since both express weaknesses that are actually anything but where work is concerned. Honestly, who's going to turn you down for a job because you aim for perfection in your work or love shouldering responsibility? Nobody! Nevertheless, this question tends to march on year after year and candidates continue to answer it as evasively as possible.

Edison's life causes me to reconsider my attitudes about this question. I won't change my mind and say that it's a great question to ask in interviews. However, I will wholeheartedly state that each and every entrepreneur needs to ask themselves this question and make a serious attempt to determine their greatest weakness. You should do so because this information just might point you toward the capitalist nirvana of competitive advantage.

E IS FOR EDISON

Key Lesson: Limit your way to greater creativity.

- What are your company's weaknesses, and which one would your competitors seek to avoid at all cost?
- Where could somebody look at your company and say "desperation, not inspiration"?
- Where can you voluntarily impose more limits on your company and motivate greater creativity?

Chapter 3

TALENT, NOT TITLES

E DISON WAS KEENLY AWARE THAT TALENT WAS NECESSARY TO build a successful organization. He was known to lament, "There is far more opportunity than there is ability." When it came time to staff his operations, Edison's primary strategy was to build an organization that attracted and kept talented people. He completely ignored titles and pedigrees. You didn't need a college or even a high school education to work for Edison. In fact, he was suspicious of people who stood behind their college credentials and completely lacked any kind of practical experience. His shop had a revolving door and anybody was welcome to drop in and try the work. If they were good, they might be asked to stick around. And if they were extremely good, Edison did his best to keep them from leaving.

Edison knew talent because he was talented. In fact, his life is peppered with stories that reflect not only his own level of talent but also how he attracted it. Let's return to Edison's early days as a migrant telegraph operator for a glimpse of his own abilities. After several years in the business he journeyed to Boston to work in one of the Western Union offices there. In the telegraph operator's labor market, Boston was second only to New York City as a center of telegraphy. Thus, it can be said that Edison was "running with the big dogs."

It was common in telegraphy culture to haze a new arrival. Edison arrived in Boston looking very much like a country boy from the Midwest because…well, he was a country boy from the Midwest and was also a bit disheveled from a long train ride. In Boston, however, the local telegraph operators fancied themselves gentlemen and dressed in the latest fashions. They most likely took Edison for a simpleton and decided to haze him appropriately before putting him to work. They arranged for him to receive a telegram from one of the fastest senders in New York City (who was also in on the joke).

Edison recognized the setup as a hazing situation almost immediately. He received the message from New York at a dizzying speed that continued to climb and the New York operator realized that Edison wasn't so simple after all. As Edison wrote the message down, the rest of the office gathered around him expecting to enjoy a laugh at his expense. The joke was to be on them, however, as Edison's talent far outstripped their rural prejudices. He quickly determined that he could stay four or five words per minute ahead of the New Yorker's fastest pace. As the New Yorker began to abbreviate to further complicate Edison's handwritten transcription of the Morse-code message, Edison interrupted the transmission and sent back the message, "You seem to be tired, suppose you send a little while with your other foot?"

By making talent his calling card, Edison shattered any false preconceptions people might have of him and established his good reputation almost immediately. There are only two choices when it comes to calling cards: talents or titles. Since he was only in his early 20s, Edison certainly didn't have any titles. Nor did he garner the official titles of college graduates since he never attended a college or university. Therefore, he established himself with his talent and built his early businesses using people with talent rather than titles.

RULE #1: START WITH ENTREPRENEURIAL TALENT

Prepare yourself for the blinding flash of the obvious: The best way to have entrepreneurial talent inside your firm is to recruit talent that has been entrepreneurial outside your firm. That is, if you hire somebody who is already entrepreneurial, you'll find it much easier to get them to be entrepreneurial when working with you.

Thomas Edison didn't suddenly become entrepreneurial when he left his rural midwestern roots in Michigan and migrated to the technological hotbed of New England. Likewise, we can't expect a move to an office in Silicon Valley to turn a risk-averse bureaucrat into an entrepreneur. The fact is that Edison showed entrepreneurial tendencies from the very beginning.

GOODBYE CAREER, HELLO OPPORTUNITY

In Edison's day, nobody ever worried about having a career because nobody had one in the sense that we know it today. The notion of a career is a relatively new invention, intentionally designed to reduce your mobility in the free market. Sounds rather un-American, doesn't it? Actually, it's quite American and worked very well in retaining talent. The managers who ran Corporate America invented the career as a way to retain talent in a competitive labor market. In fact, some economists differentiate between the external labor market and the internal labor markets within companies.

When organizations ruled the world, getting fired from a job was almost as shameful as being thrown into jail. This was because Corporate America expected you to care for your career above all else. Before the coming of Corporate America, however, it was not shameful to leave or get fired from a job. Edison was often fired from his jobs. And the reason? Most often it was because he experimented too much on the job. Whereas most workers lost jobs due to gambling, drink, or bad company, Edison lost jobs due to too much experimentation.

The young Edison began his first entrepreneurial ventures when he was barely 12-years-old. One of the earliest surviving documents known to be written by him is a copy of a letter he wrote when he was 15-years-old to a childhood friend. In this letter, he apologizes to his friend for not writing more often but offers an explanation: "I ought to have written long ere this, but my time is all taken up with my business on the cars. You sea (*sic*) that I am on the Grand Trunk road. I don't get home until ten in the evening, and have no time to write except Sundays." Of course, he signed the letter "Alva Edison."

So what did he mean by his "…business on the cars"? Fascinated with the railroads that linked his hometown to the big city of Detroit, Edison started working as a newsboy on the Grand Trunk Railroad. A newsboy walked the aisles of the train between stops and sell snacks and newspapers to the passengers. The harder a newsboy pushed his sales, the more money he made each day. Edison stayed on the job for two years—a good indication that he was more extroverted and entrepreneurial than most people give him credit for.

He not only worked his own job but also mentions in his personal writings that he employed other people. About the same time he opened a vegetable stand and a newsstand in Port Huron and shared profits with the young men he hired to attend the booths (he later closed the newsstand claiming that the boy who ran it for him "could not be trusted"). He also employed other boys to help expand his newsboy business on the trains and hired a friend to transport, via train, Port Huron vegetables to sell in the more lucrative markets in Detroit. Thus, by the time Edison was 14-years-old he had hired, fired, motivated, and managed more people than 99 percent of the college graduates of his (or our) day.

CURIOSITY DIDN'T KILL THE CAT

I recently spoke with the dean of our engineering school at Baylor University (where I'm a management professor) about what it takes to be a great engineer. He responded, "We're basically just on the lookout for people who are curious." Curiosity is often at the heart of breakthrough innovation. It got a bad name during the last century when Corporate America ruled the workplace. Everyone can quote the saying, "Curiosity killed the cat." Edison's life testifies that curiosity didn't kill the cat; instead it made him richer.

Edison was educated largely at home since he was pulled from public schools at an early age after schoolteachers complained about him being "addled"—or scatterbrained. Chances are this just meant he asked too many questions. However, Edison showed early tendencies toward a lifetime of experimentation by conducting his own chemistry experiments at home. While he probably did not have the well-equipped lab depicted in *Young Tom Edison*, archeological surveys of his boyhood home have turned up ample evidence of a chemistry lab, and he was known to have enjoyed reading chemistry books.

No one story better illustrates the centrality of curiosity to Edison's life than a letter he wrote in 1877 to none other than Charles Darwin. The ever-curious Edison told the great naturalist about some little green bugs that tended to congregate outside of his laboratory windows on hot summer evenings. He noted that these insects "…give off when bothered an exceedingly strong smell of napthalene. No difference can be detected between the odor of the insect and the crystals of napthalene except that the odor from the insects is much more powerful." He suggested to Darwin that this smell of moth balls might be a self-defense mechanism much like a skunk and that it deserved more study.

It's a testament to Edison's vision that he sought to correspond with Charles Darwin. Needless to say, Darwin was considered one of the greatest scientists alive in 1877 so the young Edison was really aiming high. More amazing still, he wrote this letter just prior to achieving worldwide fame with his invention of the phonograph. Should Darwin have taken him up on his offer to study the matter together (Darwin declined), I'm sure Edison would have welcomed the partnership.

However impressive the vision, there is something even more impressive from a talent standpoint. This story suggests that Edison was curious about

LISTEN WITH YOUR TEETH
Edison's Favorite Atom: Number 4320

In an 1890 interview, Edison gave a glimpse into how his creative mind worked. One key to his success as an innovator was his desire to experience life from as many perspectives as possible. He said that it would be great if he could command each and every atom of his body to do different tasks. For example, "…then I could say to one particular atom in me—call it atom No. 4320—'Go and be part of a rose for a while.' All the atoms could be sent off to become parts of different minerals, plants, and other substances. Then, if by just pressing a little button they could be called back together again, they would bring back their experiences while they were parts of those different substances, and I should have the benefit of the knowledge."

One way to increase your own creativity is to start experiencing life from as many perspectives as possible. Take a trip to somewhere new or spend a day in the life of your most important customer. Another way is to learn to listen to the perspectives of other people with whom you work. Think of your firm as a group of atoms that go out and experience all manner of different things. Your job as a manager is to benefit from the knowledge gained by all these different "atoms" by constantly listening to what they've learned and to pass it on to other people who need that information.

little things as well as big things. Is there anything that can help you separate the truly curious from the potential employees who act curious only during the recruiting process? I think there is. Anybody can throw around buzzwords about "reinventing business" and these same people may even have spotted a legitimate market opportunity. Yet, is there any genuine curiosity underlying these buzzwords and opportunities? Maybe, maybe not. A more reliable test is to see if a person is—like Edison—curious about the little things in addition to the big, profitable things. When you're out looking for innovative talent, try to find someone who is curious about everything—right down to the bugs that might otherwise make a summer evening more enjoyable.

GETTING BEYOND THE GAME SHOW

Most businesses use recruiting practices that are relics of Corporate America. The most notable is the interview. In many companies, the interview is like a game show where the contestant—or recruit—steps into a booth for eight hours and fields questions from the game show host—or manager. The contestant tries hard to prepare for tough questions like "What are you really looking for in a job?" or "Why do you want to work for us?" The only thing missing is a manager asking "Is that your final answer?" In the recruiting game show, one wrong answer ends the game and you're stuck with the consolation prize: a round-trip ticket to the home office with no offer at the end.

Although the interview is likely to continue as an important way of assessing social and interpersonal skills, the game show model is less and less central to the recruiting strategies of the most competitive companies. Companies that are winning the talent war are interviewing in ways that make the game show model look like the Corporate America relic that it is. Here are two alternatives: behavior-based interviewing and the analytical interview.

Accenture has been one of the most successful consulting firms over the past two decades and has attracted more than their fair share of talent. Behavior-based interviewing is one tool they have used to separate the true talent from the multitude of candidates that apply for jobs at the firm each year. Behavior-based interviewing is founded on two key ideas. First, a structured interview is better than a random, meandering one. Second, the best predictor of future behavior is past behavior.

To make behavior-based interviewing work, Accenture identifies the core behaviors they want from each of their potential recruits. They do this by considering both the culture of the firm and the strategic direction the firm is taking. Let's say that a firm values persuasiveness as a core behavior in its employees. The process of behavior-based interviewing then revolves around developing questions that challenge the candidate to identify times when they have had to persuade individuals resistant to their ideas.

An experienced behavioral interviewer will keep the conversation moving with probing questions that seek to clarify the candidate's story in its full context. Should the candidate be unable to tell stories about a time they have been persuasive, then they may not be exhibiting this core behavior. If you like the idea of behavioral interviewing you can learn more about it by getting the classic training resource, *More Than a Gut Feeling* on book, video, or audio file.

Another alternative to the traditional game show interview is the analytical interview. Some firms have started asking job applicants obscure but answerable questions to learn how they can think their way through a problem. That is, the firm will ask a question that can definitely be answered but nobody will have this information sitting in their brain. Examples of such questions would be, "What percentage of countries in Africa are members of the United Nations?" or "How many cable television subscribers are there in the United States?" Edison often used such questions to select talent. His list included questions like, "How far is it from New York to San Francisco?"; "Where does the finest cotton grow?"; and "What is the greatest depth ever reached in the ocean?"

These questions allow the recruiting firm to observe the candidate's analytical mind at work. Answers like "I have no idea" might suggest either a lack of curiosity or of analytical skills. Some candidates might give a safe response like, "Let me look that up and call you back tomorrow." Such an answer might sound good but suggests that the candidate is more concerned with getting the "right" answer rather than going through an analytical process.

A truly analytical candidate might have no idea about the answer but starts off with, "I remember that the recently released U.S. Census data said that there were about 280 million Americans and if the average home has three people and we assume that at least 80 percent of homes have cable then..." Whether or not the candidate's final answer is right is beside the point. Listening to the answer, you've learned that this candidate starts with credible data (the U.S. Census), makes his assumptions explicit ("...at least 80 percent of homes have cable..."), and goes after his solution in a mathematical fashion.

Another form of this type of questioning is to ask a question that demands a decisive answer, then watch how the candidate arrives at that answer. In many ways, Microsoft pioneered this type of interviewing with questions like, "If you could remove any of the 50 states, which would it be and why?" Unlike the above questions, there's no single "right" answer but the question challenges recruits to a) give a clear answer, and b) justify it. Such questions go well beyond the canned answers of the game show model of recruiting and give valuable insight into how job candidates arrive at and defend conclusions.

SO WHAT IF THEY DON'T LIKE ME?

Thomas Edison was born into a despised ethnic group—the Dutch. His great-grandfather, John Edeson, emigrated from the Netherlands to America at the age of three with his widowed mother. He went on to settle in New Jersey and become a true "Jersey Dutchman" before having to flee to Canada during the Revolutionary War. Years later, John Edeson's great-grandson, Thomas Edison, proudly claimed his Dutch heritage by accepting an invitation to join the Holland Society of New York. Edison was Dutch and that meant that business was in his blood. Here's a little history to back up that last statement.

The Dutch were remarkably good businessmen during the Colonial Era of world history and their business acumen is still alive and well today. Some of the largest and most competitive global powerhouses are based in the

Netherlands: Royal Dutch/Shell, Unilever, and Philips, to name just a few. The trivia buffs among us know that the global paragon of finance and capitalism—New York City—was originally founded as a Dutch settlement and once called New Amsterdam. The Dutch also invented the Dutch Auction which starts with a high price and then lowers that price until somebody bids, rather than starting low and trying to push the price higher through competitive bidding (the English Auction).

Despite their business skills, or possibly because of them, the Dutch became a despised minority in a world increasingly dominated by their chief rivals, the English. This hatred grew exponentially during trade rivalries between the English and Dutch in the 17th-century. In fact, no stronger words of refusal could be uttered by a 17th- or 18th-century Englishman than "I'd rather be a Dutchman!"

The unpopularity of the Dutch among the English can be best explained by the phrase "Dutch treat." Most of us use it regularly but few of us realize that it began as an ethnic slur coined to make fun of the Dutch and their business practices. "Dutch treat" basically means that everybody pays their own way when a group goes out to dinner. Thus, a "Dutch treat" is really no treat at all and was originally a derogatory reference to somebody "too cheap to pick up the tab." Other business-related slurs included "Dutch bargain" (a one-sided deal), "Dutch books" (poor accounting), and "Dutch reckoning" (any increase in price). The racist overtones begin to show when you see some of the other slurs associated with the Dutch. A "Dutch blessing" was a beating or a whipping. "Dutch courage" was a reference to any kind of hard liquor. And to illustrate the extent of the hate involved, a prostitute was often referred to as a "Dutch widow."

Like it or not, this was Edison's heritage and a bias he faced every time he wanted to do business. Even though this may sound like an overstatement by 21st-century standards, there were strong ethnic biases among Caucasians at this point in American history. In fact, I suspect these biases could be at the heart of many of the myths about Edison being a bad businessman. As with all racism, the Dutch were ridiculed on the business front because they were successful and the only way their foes could feel better about themselves was to insult the Dutch.

In spite of these anti-Dutch biases, Edison succeeded because he worked hard and delivered on his promises. He had talent, period. His early successes taught him that talent and passion alone mattered because the free market was unprejudiced as to one's ethnicity and was results-oriented. If some gatekeeper did not like your background and rejected your ideas because of it then it was his loss in the long-run.

THE MORNING AFTER?

Most of us like to have our picture taken when we're looking our best. Thomas Edison was no different and that's why he once insisted that he have his picture made after he had gone three days without sleep. If you've never had the chance to see what some-body looks like after three days without sleep then take a good look at this picture. Edison honored inspiration at any cost and sleep was often one of the first casualties.

Whereas most photos attempt to commemorate people looking their best, this photo captures Edison looking his absolute worst. Nevertheless, right next to him on the table sits a working phonograph. Maybe the photo

A PHOTO OF EDISON TAKEN WHEN HE HAD WORKED FOR THREE DAYS WITHOUT SLEEP IN AN EFFORT TO PRODUCE AN IMPROVED PHONOGRAPH.
(Photo courtesy of U.S. Department of the Interior, National Park Service, Edison National Historic Site)

captures Edison at his best, after all. Edison liked this photo so much that he commissioned a portrait from it that now hangs in his library and office at the Edison National Historic Site. You can actually view this portrait online at www.nps. gov/edis/virtual tour/library/portrait.htm. The portrait is titled "The Napoleon of Invention" in light of Edison's resemblance to him in this portrait and also because few technological challenges could withstand continued assaults by Edison. If nothing else, this photo reminds me to judge talent by its accomplishments rather than its looks.

FIXING A BUM TICKER

Before the coming of the game-show interview, work-sample tests were a common way to assess the skills of potential employees. In a work-sample test, a potential employee must do something they would do every day on the job—like repairing a broken machine. Edison made talent his calling card and was no stranger to the work-sample test.

During his time as a telegraph operator, Edison applied at the Western Union company for an operator position. Western Union owned and operated miles of telegraph wire and was one of the first multistate corporations to appear in America. When I say "applied" this means that he sat in the waiting room at the Western Union office for a few days during which time he had the chance to thoroughly study the stock market tickers and message senders that connected the office to the floor of the Gold Exchange and other trading offices in the financial district.

During the third day of his waiting period, the main message-sending machine made what he called "a very great noise, [and] suddenly came to a stop with a crash." Almost immediately, message boys from every broker on the street began to appear in the already crowded waiting room announcing that their stock ticker was broken and that it must be fixed at once. A general panic ensued as up to 300 message boys began to crowd into a room built for only 100 people, all demanding immediate attention and action. According to

WHAT'S YOUR BAG?

Austin, Texas is definitely a cool place to live and work and one of the coolest places to go in Austin is Amy's Ice Cream. As cool as Amy's might be, the company faces a huge talent problem. Austin's high-tech industry sucks up the available labor force like a vacuum offering wages at three times minimum wage to completely untrained workers. Then there's that slacker thing. How do you avoid getting stuck with an unmotivated employee in the city that invented the term "slacker" to describe the aimless, motionless lifestyle profiled in Richard Linklater's appropriately titled cult film *Slacker*?

Amy's Ice Cream stumbled across a great solution and it all started by accident when the company ran out of job applications. On that fateful day, the company started giving out plain, white paper bags to job applicants with two words of instruction: "Be creative." The results have been fabulous. Simple, white paper bags have been transformed into works of art, tiny replicas of Amy's Ice Cream stores, masks, and containers to hold everything from photo essays to custom-made videotapes.

Amy Miller, CEO of Amy's Ice Creams, Inc., believes that going out for ice cream should be the high point of her customer's day and a totally wonderful experience. Her bag test quickly identifies dynamic people who share her core value of creating fabulousness out of the ordinary. This accidental talent screen goes a long way toward ensuring that Amy's customers will be taken care of by workers that can make something wonderful out of the most ordinary thing imaginable: a plain paper bag.

Edison, the manager in charge of the room seemed paralyzed and couldn't overcome his own panic enough to respond to the situation. Fortunately, Edison had been studying the instrument for several days as he waited for his job opportunity and had noticed that one of the many springs that ran the instrument had come loose and fallen down between two of the gear wheels, effectively jamming the instrument. As Edison approached the man in charge of the room to tell him the nature of the problem, an owner from one of the broker houses that subscribed to Western Union's service, Samuel Laws, appeared on the scene and angrily demanded to know the cause of the trouble.

The manager was speechless and Edison turned to the agitated Mr. Laws and said he knew what the problem was. The owner responded, "Fix it, fix it, be quick." Edison did, and the message boys slowly began dispersing throughout the financial district to reset the machines in their offices. Things returned to normal within about two hours. Mr. Laws then asked Edison what he happened to be doing at the Western Union office. Edison told him, and Laws asked him to drop by his office the next day.

It turned out that Laws was the owner of the Gold and Stock Indicator Company and a man of no small influence and learning. Laws talked at length with Edison about his knowledge of stock tickers and other instruments and offered Edison a job with his company. Edison took the job and managed to make several improvements on Laws' machines and systems until he moved on to another job.

NEW KINDS OF WORK-SAMPLE TESTS

The above story shows that there's nothing like a work-sample test to identify true talent. Best of all, the only question you need to ask as part of such a test is, "How much will it take to get you to join our firm?" The work-sample test is making a comeback but it's less and less a matter of fixing broken products. Modern work-sample tests are designed to identify talent suited for today's knowledge-driven, service-oriented economy.

Enron, the self-proclaimed market-making laboratory of innovation uses this type of talent screen in their information technology area. Should you wonder about Enron's claim, keep in mind that in 2000 *Fortune* magazine named them the most innovative company in the world and ranked them as one of the top ten companies in America in their ability to attract, develop, and retain great talent. One way Enron assesses talent is to have a candidate's future peers watch the candidate complete a sample job task. In a service company like Enron, such a peer-evaluated exercise is one-half interview and one-half work sample.

Working at a university a mere four hours north-northwest of Enron's headquarters in Houston, I have several students each semester sign on with the company and some of them give some pretty amazing reports. Recently, a student accepted a job in their information technology area and talked to me about his selection process. As part of the talent screen, he and his fellow recruits were asked to create an implementation plan for a particular kind of Web site. To do this, they had to interview their interviewers at Enron (who played the role of the client) to ascertain what exactly was needed. A big part of the selection process is watching which candidates take a leadership role and which recruits ask the right kind of questions. A bit of a reversal from hoping that the recruits give the right kind of answers, eh?

The consulting firm McKinsey & Company also uses a modified work sample to assess talent. Before you work at McKinsey, you have to solve a case. McKinsey offers job applicants sample cases on their Web site. When an applicant interviews at McKinsey, the hiring partners watch closely how the applicant frames the problem and what questions the applicant asks to obtain more information. At McKinsey, it's not so much a process of arriving at the "right" answer—that's the old game-show model of interviewing. Rather, it's a process of watching the candidate arrive at their answer and determining whether or not they are the kind of person that can view long-standing problems in new, frame-breaking ways.

WORTH HANGING AROUND FOR

Speaking of McKinsey & Company, they released a report recently that suggested that the most talented people in the new economy are like frogs in a wheelbarrow—they can jump out at any time. To keep this from happening, McKinsey & Company suggested developing a killer Employee Value Proposition—or EVP. In other words, what do you have that makes your employee want to stick around? The old notion of "don't move because you have a great career here" just doesn't seem to be doing it anymore.

Edison had an EVP when it came to keeping the employees he believed were too valuable to lose. At Edison's labs, anybody was welcome to walk through the door and try their hand at inventing as long as they paid for the supplies and equipment that they used. If they were good, they might be invited to join the lab as a "mucker." Muckers worked hard and slowly ascended a ladder of better paying and more important jobs. At the top of this ladder was Edison and his boys who shared handsomely in the profits from all of the inventions in the lab. For an ambitious young inventor in the late 19th century it's hard to know which of the two EVPs held more value—sharing invention royalties or working side-by-side with Edison.

The goal of an EVP is to increase the probability of your most wanted talent staying with you. Of course, there are stock options but they're so common now that they don't need an explanation. Other EVPs include large blocks of sabbatical or vacation time that employees can structure into their work contracts. Such time is especially important in firms that rely heavily on innovation. Top talent at such firms might find it beneficial to have a three-month block of vacation time every few years. Another popular EVP is company-provided technology including laptops, cellular phones, personal digital assistants, high-speed Internet access at home, and just about any other technological toy you can imagine.

One of the most remarkable EVPs is the Clara Abbott Scholarship Fund for employees at Abbott Laboratories. Abbott Labs is a pharmaceutical and healthcare product company founded by Wallace Abbott in the late 1800s. The scholarship fund was named in honor of his wife, Clara. This fund provides money for tuition, fees, books, and supplies for children and dependents of Abbott Lab employees at colleges and vocational schools. To put it simply, this remarkable benefit makes it possible for employees at Abbott Labs to significantly reduce the cost of going to college.

The scholarship application takes about 15 minutes to complete and scholarships are awarded based upon financial need. Despite the fact that a university or vocational education can be a great investment in human capital, post-secondary education can still be out of reach for many people given the high cost of tuition and fees. Imagine the benefit that accrues to a top-notch lab worker at Abbott Labs with three college-aged children. It's conceivable that the scholarship program could pay out upwards of $200,000 of benefits to the employee. Better still, neither the employee nor the children are saddled with loans for decades after they finish school. Everybody wins: It's a great tax write-off for the company and the employee doesn't have to figure out how to save money for their child's college education.

HOW ABOUT "LUNCH AT NO ADDITIONAL COST TO YOU"?

You may have heard the oft-quoted line, "There's no free lunch." In the most abstract economic sense this might be true—we can't consume what we don't produce. However, there is a place you can work where you can have lunch every working day at no additional cost to yourself. That place is known as Hewitt Associates and it's one of the largest human resource management consultants in the United States.

Hewitt Associates was founded in 1940 by Ted Hewitt to help business executives and other professionals in financial planning. Hewitt's original core business was insurance brokering but it soon evolved into a firm that provides benefit services to major employers in the United States. Today, Hewitt provides comprehensive services for large employers who wish to outsource the administration of their health and retirement benefits.

Hewitt's "free lunch" program goes by the more official name of "On-Site Food Service." It is both good business and good for talent retention. And why is it working? Well, for starters, hardly anybody else offers it. Other firms may have low-priced employee cafeterias—but they're low-priced, not free. Depending on how much you spend on lunch each day, a free lunch can save you between $1,500 to $2,000 each year. Second, free lunches keep people onsite talking with one another and accessible to clients. If you get enough people talking around enough tables, you get some fabulous ideas. In Edison's shop, lots of people gathered around the workbench and talked about creative ways to solve their problems. The same thing can happen around the lunch table—especially when there's a free lunch.

Just in case you want to copy this model, here are a few tips I learned from Hewitt employees. First, lunch might be free but desserts are restricted to only certain days of the week. Second, almost every Hewitt site sponsors a Weight Watchers program in addition to its free lunch program. Hewitt also offers a free breakfast service in the mornings and a free snack service in the afternoons as well as a Starbucks coffee bar in many locations. Some of Hewitt's other innovative employee benefits include overnight care for pets when associates are traveling on company business and "splash" time—big blocks of additional vacation time during your employment anniversary years. For example, you get an additional two weeks of vacation during your tenth year with the company. These big blocks of time off allow associates the flexibility they might need to plan an extra special, extra long vacation with family and friends.

These days, we're only beginning to lift the lid off the free market approach to talent that ruled America prior to the coming of Corporate America. By now you should have a good understanding of the important role that talent played in Edison's success and some tools to help you identify the best available talent in the marketplace. Remember that the idea of a "career" is a relic from Corporate America and something that needs to be reconsidered as you continue to make the transition to Post-Corporate America.

E IS FOR EDISON

Key Lesson: Talent comes and talent goes but mediocrity accumulates.

- What are you doing to move beyond the game-show model of interviewing?
- Does your company have a revolving door for talent?
- Who would you consider your core talent? What are you doing to make them want to stay rather than leave?

Chapter 4

GET CONNECTED

O NE OF THE GREAT MYTHS ABOUT THOMAS EDISON was that he was just a really lucky fellow. In fact, one of his biographers titled his book *A Streak of Luck*, suggesting that Edison relied on luck to save him. No, inventing was hard work for Edison and success was not lucky or accidental. He addressed this in an 1880s interview in *Harper's* magazine when he said:

> *It is too often the fashion to attribute all inventions to accident, and a great deal of nonsense is talked on this score. In my own case, but few, and those the least important, of my inventions owed anything to accident. Most of them had been hammered out after long and patient labor, and are the result of countless experiments, all directed toward attaining some well-defined object.*

Edison worked and he worked hard. He also believed there to be a difference between the act of invention and the act of discovery. Invention occurred when he had a preexisting vision for the thing that he was going to invent, like the light bulb. Although it took a while to perfect, Edison always carried a clear picture of what the light bulb would look like and how it would work. He may have invented the light bulb but he claimed that he discovered the phonograph. Discovery, in contrast to invention, was when you had no vision for a particular item and stumbled across it on your way to somewhere else.

For the phonograph, this "somewhere else" was the automatic telegraph. Edison spent his early years working as a telegraph operator sending and receiving messages. As a result, his busy mind was always at work trying to invent ways to make the operator's job easier. The idea behind the automatic telegraph was simple. Whenever a new message came in, the automatic telegraph would convert the dots and dashes of the Morse code into holes on a long strip of paper. The message was then permanently captured on this paper and could be fed through a machine that read the dots and dashes and sent them down the line to the next station. The automatic telegraph was revolutionary in that it significantly increased the speed with which messages were both received and sent.

When the message was sent down the line through the automatic telegraph, the dots and dashes sounded like human voices as they beeped through the machine at speeds per minute far exceeding what humans had ever been able to send. Even with his loss of hearing, Edison recognized the similarity of this sound with the human voice and began to visualize a machine that could go beyond capturing the binary dots and dashes and capture more complex sounds like the human voice. Best of all, once the voice was captured, it could be played back for generations to come. Thus, the idea of the phonograph was born while Edison was on the road to somewhere else.

Creativity is all about making connections and Edison was a great innovator because he was great at making connections. Just as the phonograph was connected to the telegraph, many of Edison's inventions were connected to one another. For example, he described the invention of the motion picture as doing for the eye what the phonograph did for the ear. Edison relied heavily upon personal experience in stimulating him toward greater creativity, but there are other ways to make connections and increase creativity. Here we'll discuss four tools for making connections: science, personal experience, record keeping, and—believe it or not—poetry.

MAKING CONNECTIONS WITH SCIENCE

Science is all about making new connections. The scientific process involves documenting, in the most objective way possible, that this is related to that—for example, that aerobic exercise is related to health. Corporate research and development groups are an extension of the scientific process and exist to make new connections through formal programs of research, like documenting that certain pharmaceuticals are related to certain healing processes. The heart of science is theory and there are three main uses for theory:

Theory is used to explain. Theory is a simple story about how a complex world works. If we want to explain to our children why there are no more dinosaurs, we reach for theory. Nobody alive today was around when the dinosaurs died out. Nonetheless, we might start our story with, "Well son, this big meteor slammed into the earth and caused the climate to change dramatically and..." We weren't there. We didn't witness the events. But theory helps us to explain things.

We use theory all the time in business, too. It helps us answer a variety of questions such as, "Why do some companies make more money than other companies?" or "Why do some employees achieve more than other employees?" Well-known theories like Michael Porter's Five Forces theory or Edwin Locke's goal-setting theory might help us explain a pattern of events to somebody else.

Theory is used to predict. When we explain, we are talking about the past. When we predict, we are talking about the future. You are probably making use of some kind of theory every time you hire a new employee. Most of us have implicit theories that guide our hiring activities and decisions. For example, if we believe that past behavior is the best predictor of future behavior, then our hiring process will revolve around understanding how our applicants behaved in the past. This is the heart of the behavior-based interviewing process at places like Accenture.

THEORY IGNORES THE MISFIT

Given that theory is used to explain, predict, and control, what do you do with the data that doesn't fit? Well, it typically gets thrown away. Research scientists collect vast amounts of evidence to verify the truth of their theories. A typical research finding will trumpet, "…and 87 percent of the data fell into the proper categories." But what about that other 13 percent? It might get ignored in a research lab but it didn't in Edison's invention labs. His lab notebooks are full of unexplained observations or "misfits" that deserved further investigation.

For example, a rather technical entry from February 2, 1877, reads, "Phenonmenon: if a piece of metallic silicon is placed between two metallic or carbon poles and manipulated so as to get it red hot, a continuous electric light with snaps is obtained." Hmmm…and this was well over a year before he announced his intention to develop an electric light bulb. Theory can be very useful but it can limit your options, too. Edison successfully brought a number of observational misfits to life by keeping track of "phenomena" or observations that didn't fit the traditional or theoretical explanations. "Recognize" and "record" were his two operative words. Sometimes he would get back to the misfit and sometimes he wouldn't. If business is about noticing opportunities that others do not, a good place to begin looking is among the misfits.

If we didn't have theories about the future, then we may as well draw lots to determine which applicants get hired and which do not. That's because we hope theory helps us beat the 50-50 odds of hiring a bad employee. Likewise, many blackjack players utilize probability theory when they play the game.

Counting and remembering which cards have been played helps some players better predict when to bet more money on the next cards dealt.

Theory is used to control. One of the most common uses of theory in business is to exert control over programs of research in large organizations. For example, let's say a large pharmaceutical company decides to develop a drug that dramatically slows down the aging process. Needless to say, millions of

PERFECTLY RATIONAL FORECASTS

If you remain unconvinced of the danger of complete rationality grounded in good theory, consider the evidence of some of these perfectly rational decisions made by perfectly rational business-people using perfectly rational forecasts:

- "Sorry, Mr. Epstein, but groups with guitars are on the way out." (A Decca Records executive turning down Beatles manager Brian Epstein.)
- "There will never be a bigger plane built." (A Boeing engineer after the first flight of the 247, a twin-engine plane that carried ten people.)
- "With over 50 foreign cars already on sale here, the Japanese auto industry isn't likely to carve out a big slice of the U.S. market." (*Business Week*, August 2, 1968)
- "There is no reason anyone would want a computer in their home." (Ken Olsen, President of Digital Equipment Corp., 1977)
- "Who wants to hear actors talk?" (H.M. Warner, Warner Brothers, 1927)
- "Stocks have reached a permanently high plateau." (Irving Fisher, Professor of Economics, Yale University, 1929)

dollars will be funneled into such a research effort. The management of the pharmaceutical company is accountable for the dollars spent on such research, so they will want to exert control over the research process in an effort to minimize the waste. Therefore, some type of theory about the aging process will guide the allocation of resources in the experimental labs. This theory will set boundaries around the investigation, frame the sorts of questions to be answered, and generally restrict and channel the activities of the employees working on the problem. This sounds rather sinister but ends up making good economic sense.

NO EXPERTS IN THE UNKNOWN

One long-standing myth about Edison was that he was a great scientist. However, the fact is that Edison was not your average scientist. He considered himself a scientist whose job it was to apply scientific knowledge to solve human problems, specifically by creating consumer products and services. This is not a popular job description among what Edison called "pure scientists." Most pure scientists seek knowledge for knowledge's sake rather than for commercial application. In fact, The National Academy of Sciences in America voted down his first nomination in 1911 and only grudgingly admitted him to membership in 1927—four years before his death.

Unlike most scientists, Edison never created for the sake of scientific discovery. He stated, "I do not regard myself as a pure scientist, as so many persons have insisted that I am. I do not search for the laws of nature, and have made no great discoveries of such laws. I do not study science as Newton or Farraday and Henry studied it, simply for the purpose of learning truth. I am only a professional inventor. My studies and experiments have been conducted *entirely with the object of inventing that which will have commercial utility.*" In other words, invention was a business for Edison. He only created products that he believed could be turned into successful businesses and the scientific community despised him for it.

When it came to innovation, Edison didn't put a lot of trust in theory. In fact, he often found theory to be like a set of blinders that keep you from seeing all possible solutions. Competitors, like fellow electrical pioneer Nikola Tesla, harshly criticized Edison regarding his views. In an interview, Tesla captured the essence of Edison's method when he said, "If [Edison] had a needle to find in a haystack, he would not stop to reason where it was most likely to be, he would proceed at once with the feverish diligence of the bee to examine straw after straw until he found the object of his search. His method was inefficient in the extreme, for an immense ground had to be covered to get anything at all unless blind chance intervened, and at first I was almost a sorry witness of his doings, knowing that just a little theory and calculation would have saved him 90 percent of the labor. But he has a veritable contempt for book learning and mathematical knowledge, trusting himself entirely to his inventor's instinct and practical American sense."

Tesla was almost the complete opposite of Edison when it came to innovation and his comments seem to be straight out of Corporate America. Although Tesla worked for Edison for a while, they ultimately parted ways after a series of misunderstandings and it's not hard to see why, given Tesla's disdain for the "inefficient" Edison. Edison was also the opposite of Tesla and knew there was absolutely no theory that would help him know where exactly to start looking for the needle in the haystack. His problem with theory was that he understood very well that there are no experts on the unknown.

Despite his comments to the contrary, Edison didn't have a complete disdain for science and theory. He eventually learned to accommodate the academics in their white lab coats. Although he hired formally educated people to work for him, he deplored formal education. He believed it ruined your ability to think. To Edison, the ABC's of education stood for "Avoid Being Creative." Although he understood the theories of his day, he found them useless in solving unknown problems like capturing sound or creating motion pictures. Theory and Corporate America went hand-in-hand. Corporate America wanted efficiency, standardization, and control and theory fit the bill perfectly. Theory gave Corporate America the power to explain what had happened, boldly predict the future, and control and coordinate the actions of subordinates and divisions. As a result, business schools all over America began teaching classes in management theory and organizational theory. Corporate America would discover that theory was nice but it didn't keep things from changing. The world in which Corporate America thrived started to change and their theory didn't stop it from happening.

Post-Corporate America has wised up to the idea of charging ahead into the unknown even when there's no theory to guide you. As a result, we've witnessed the rise of data mining as a legitimate business practice. In academic circles where theory rules as absolute monarch, data mining is just short of career suicide. In the marketplace, however, resources to help business owners best leverage their ever-growing databases have exploded. Sometimes data mining masquerades as the more respectable practice of customer relationship management—or CRM. In the past couple of years, books have hit the market with titles like *Data Mining: Concepts and Techniques* and *The Data Mining Cookbook: Modeling Data for Marketing, Risk, and Customer Relationship Management.* Even the prestigious Harvard Business School has started to mention data mining in their publications including the subtly titled book *Net Worth: Shaping Markets When Customers Make the Rules.* Furthermore, dozens of consulting firms now specialize in data mining and data-mining services have emerged at some of the biggest, most prestigious consulting firms in the marketplace like KPMG and Accenture—although they might masquerade under the more professional-sounding name "Customer Management."

Data mining has emerged as a legitimate business practice as businesses have crossed into unknown customer territory. Our basic ability to capture data about transactions with customers has changed dramatically since the advent of e-commerce and large-scale data warehousing applications from firms like Oracle. Currently, firms like Amazon.com can keep track of not only everything you order but every item you browse through at their site.

They now use this data to push products toward you in the sidebars of their Web page, hoping that you'll find them interesting. Since nobody has ever had this much data on customers and customers have never shopped this way before, old but proven theories might help you make some sense of the data but you might miss some critical relationships. Therefore, more and more companies are starting with the data to draw conclusions about the customer rather than the other way around. When there are no experts in the unknown, trust the most informed player in the game: the customer.

ARE YOU EXPERIENCED?

In a 1926 interview in *The Forum* magazine, Edison expressed his skepticism toward college degrees in light of the harsh realities of the competitive marketplace. He said:

> *Business is a college more exacting than any of the schools and universities which make up what we call our educational system. Its courses are strictly practical and its teachers are what men of this generation describe as 'hard boiled,' but it is a school, a college, or a university as the student of its compulsory education may elect. Its courses are not always free. For some of the instruction all of us pay very high tuition. Only to a certain extent are they elective. That only a small percentage of the young men of today adapt themselves effectively to such of them as they choose and pass their examinations for promotion with high standing is sufficient indication that general preparation for their requirements is far from ideal. That is where there is greatest room for real improvement in our education. When we consider it as an actual preparation for the hard, cold, delightful, warm, inevitable experiences of actual life we shall have developed it to just about its limit.*

When blazing a trail into the unknown, Edison's life showed us that experience often beat theory in the race to bring an innovation to the marketplace. Edison enjoyed looking at life from as many perspectives as possible. He believed the broader your knowledge and experience base, the better your ability to solve problems. To him, the best knowledge was experience-

MAKING CONNECTIONS AT IDEO

If there's a company that has come closest to recreating Edison's creative output in modern times, it's the Silicon-valley design firm IDEO. IDEO is the company behind Apple's first mouse, the Palm V handheld computer, and a host of other hit products. In fact, the *San Francisco Examiner* reported in 1994, "IDEO of Palo Alto has designed more of the things at our fingertips than practically anyone else in the past 100 years, with the possible exception of Thomas Edison." Like Edison, IDEO is able to succeed at this level because of its ability to make connections.

IDEO works hard to create connections throughout their business. Founder David Kelley realized that one of his most important roles is to increase the number of interactions among his workers. Kelley states, "I'm the person who builds the stage rather than performs on it." As such, IDEO optimized its office design to maximize interactions among employees by using video cameras to track existing traffic patterns. They then redesigned their offices to increase employee interaction.

IDEO also has what's known as the Tech Box, a company-wide "shoebox" of curious gadgets and cutting-edge products that workers can play with whenever they wish. Furthermore, IDEO has been known to send their people on field trips to place like the Barbie Hall of Fame and the Robot Wars where robots fight to the "death" to prove engineering supremacy.

based knowledge. That's why he steered away from college-trained workers and sought out people with machine-shop experience who knew which end of the wrench to hold. He believed that inventing involved a tacit dimension that could never be learned as a student but must be experienced as an apprentice—or "mucker" as he called it. As a result, he relied on muckers far more than college graduates.

In the machine-shop culture of Pre-Corporate America, experience was one of the most important things you could bring through the door. *All* capital in Pre-Corporate America was knowledge capital—or, rather, "know-how" capital—in contrast to the "check your brains at the door" mentality that dominated Corporate America. In Corporate America, credentials in the form of a union card or college degree were necessary for entry into the corporation. In Pre-Corporate America, experience was everything.

Machine-shop culture of Edison's day was grounded in the ancient notion of the master and apprentice. That is, you learned by doing and then were commissioned to go and teach this knowledge to other people. The machine shop culture that flourished around the workbenches in Edison's labs was a vast, mutually-owned storehouse of knowledge—like a living library. Nowadays, all this knowledge is written down and stored in libraries and online for anybody's use. In those days, there was no library—just people who moved from place to place and shared ideas with one another.

Experience may also be at the heart of intuition. The idea of intuition has reached rather mythical proportions and is believed by some to be a magical power that some people—like Edison—have and others do not. Systematic studies of intuition tell a very different story, however. Gary Klein, author of the book *Sources of Power*, has studied intuition for decades. His research suggests that people who "intuitively" make great decisions under extreme circumstances are often subconsciously drawing upon an experience base that helps them recognize a successful path through dangerous territory.

In addition to other groups, Klein and his team studied firefighters and emergency room personnel who had to make critical, often life-saving decisions within a matter of seconds. Klein and his colleagues were able to demystify intuition and demonstrate that better decision makers often have a large base of experience to draw upon. This experience also often leads to "breakthrough" decisions that solve problems or save lives in unexpected ways.

Personal experience is so important to discovery that at least one college in America is giving credit where credit is due: The Thomas Edison State College in Trenton, New Jersey. Chartered by the State of New Jersey in 1972, this college was the first in the nation devoted to the idea of giving experienced adults the opportunity to get credits toward a degree by demonstrating the knowledge equivalent to classroom learning. It pioneered a number of meth-

"WWW.CONNECTWITHCUSTOMERS.COM"

One of the great Internet companies to emerge in the 90s was www.edmunds.com which makes connections between customers and providers of all kinds of services related to vehicle purchases. Edmunds.com began as a paperback guidebook for people wanting to purchase automobiles. As technologies developed, the company tried an interactive CD-ROM version of its buyer's guide. The CD-ROM flopped but Edmunds decided to download the files on the newly emerged World Wide Web.

Edmunds quickly realized that it had a popular Web site on its hands. Vehicle buyers could now log onto the Web from home and gather volumes of information to help them navigate their new and used vehicle purchases. In response, Edmunds began partnerships with insurance, loan, and aftermarket accessory companies and placed links to these firms directly from the Edmunds site. It made its revenue by successfully referring consumers to these other Web sites.

ods of documenting college-level knowledge that adults may have but just don't have a diploma to show for it. Their mission and message are clear: experience is education. In 1992, the college awarded its namesake, Thomas Edison, a bachelor of science degree in applied science and technology. At the award ceremony, the president of the college stressed that the degree was not honorary but rather was earned by Edison.

THE POWER OF DOODLING

Part of Edison's legacy is approximately five million papers documenting his life as an inventor and businessman. Edison didn't develop the habit of keeping systematic records of his inventions until 1871. Prior to that, however, he kept paper and notebooks handy to maintain records of experiments, draw diagrams, and record ideas when they came to him. In October 1870 he concluded a pocket notebook with the notation, "all new inventions I will here after keep a full record." For the most part, he kept his word on this promise.

Edison's mind was an open book and much of his writing was captured in the journals that populated every corner of his labs at Menlo Park and West Orange. He and his boys left behind around 3,500 notebooks containing literally millions of sheets of paper that are housed at the Edison National Historic Site. Edison was a fanatic about writing down every idea that came to him. In 1871, 30 years before Orville and Wilbur Wright made their historic flight at Kittyhawk, Edison penned these thoughts in a notebook: "[an] engine can be so constructed of steel and with hollow magnets…and combined with suitable air propelling apparatus wings…as to produce a flying machine of extreme lightness and tremendous power."

The notebook might well have been the most important piece of equipment in his labs. Edison and his boys recorded their inspirations in these notebooks as well as their failures. So why aren't there any books authored by Edison? The answer is that he didn't write as much as he drew things. From time to time, he experienced moments of inspiration where he clearly saw the solution to the problem he had been wrestling with. Whenever this happened, he quickly found one of his ever-present notebooks and outlined the solution in as much detail as possible, including illustrations. Sometimes this inspiration worked the first time—as with the phonograph—and sometimes it took months of perfecting—as with the light bulb.

Some of this was driven by concerns that a patent lawsuit might demand evidence of the exact date that Edison arrived at a new concept. Another explanation was that the notebooks were the equivalent of a company-wide Intranet where workers could go to pick up new ideas, read about previous experiments and failures, and leave their reaction. Edison and his boys often returned to the notebooks to follow up on items that were noted as "promising" but couldn't be acted upon in the heat of the current experiment. Beyond legal considerations, the most important thing to emerge from the culture of note taking that dominated Edison's labs was the increased number of connections. The ever-present notebooks provided a means to record fleeting but important ideas and then to return at a later time to connect all the pieces.

These documents have, in turn, helped us make new connections about Edison's life and business practices. Over the years, he accumulated an incredible number of documents that chronicle in detail the activities surrounding many of his inventions and the management of his companies. Among these papers are his personal correspondence, experimental notebooks, a variety of technical notes and drawings, his patent records, various scrapbooks, and numerous documents detailing his business operations. After his passing in 1931, these documents remained associated with his companies until they were donated to the National Park Service in 1957. They have been maintained since then at the Edison National Historical Site in West Orange, New Jersey.

In the late 1970s, Rutgers, the State University of New Jersey, spearheaded an effort to catalogue the Edison Papers for the purpose of making them accessible for study. The results of their efforts have revolutionized our heretofore limited understanding of Edison's inventive nature and business practices. Interestingly enough, the effort to sort through these papers has been anything but an ivory tower academic exercise. For years, researchers and archivists had to work in the non-air-conditioned buildings of the West Orange laboratory complex. Furthermore, they worked on Edison's original chemical-saturated tables and were often shocked to find rashes developing on the parts of their bodies that came into contact with these furnishings.

One of the most significant things this undertaking did was to banish the myth of Edison as a second-rate businessman. Andre Millard's 1990 book *Edison and the Business of Innovation* demonstrates persuasively that Edison was not the business bungler he was made out to be in earlier, less informed biographies. Millard grounds his research in numerous, previously unavailable documents that give great insight into the management of Edison's empire of invention. Likewise, Paul Israel's 1998 archive-driven biography *Edison: A Life of Invention* reveals Edison as less of a mythical wizard and more of a deliberate, creative businessman.

The Edison Papers project will continue to make more material available over the next two decades. As a result, our views on Edison and his business of innovation will continue to evolve. To date, four volumes of *The Papers of Thomas A. Edison* have been published in book form and 15 to 20 volumes are expected. One-quarter of a million pages have been converted to microfilm and a great deal of information is also available at the Web site edison.rutgers.edu.

MAKING CONNECTIONS WITH POETRY

Edison loved poetry and found it a great source of personal motivation and creative inspiration. Henry Wadsworth Longfellow's epic poem *Evangeline* was one of his favorite books. More surprisingly, Edison was known to have penned a few lines of his own poetry. He once said, "Inventors must be poets so that they may have imagination." In other words, he suggests that reading and writing poetry may be one of the best things you can do to become a more innovative businessperson. So what is the link between creativity and poetry? Well, it all goes back to a guy named Aristotle.

LISTEN WITH YOUR TEETH
Write Your Own Autobiography

Creativity is about making connections and connections are often made on paper. You've already learned that Edison kept very detailed journals about his work activities, but he also had a variety of other writings including essays, poetry, a science magazine, a personal diary, and even an abandoned science-fiction novel. He also took a brief stab at writing his autobiography but ultimately turned the project over to his "official" biographers Frank Dyer and Thomas Martin. Edison isn't alone in his endeavor to write his own life story. Other business luminaries like Benjamin Franklin, P.T. Barnum, Henry Ford, Berry Gordy, Jr., Lee Iacocca, and Mary Kay Ash have written autobiographies.

Numerous creativity consultants recommend writing your autobiography as one of the first steps toward becoming a more creative person. The process of reflecting on your life and writing it down will cause you to make connections between people and events that you might never have noticed before. Rather than opening a new document in your word processor and waiting for inspiration to strike, why not start with a simple daily journal or diary? Keep track of the significant events and experiences that shape your life and work. In addition, start jotting down significant memories from your past. After you've kept the journal for a year, use it as the foundation for an autobiography.

Writing about your life and work will give you a new perspective about yourself and the forces that shape your world. If creativity is really all about making connections then the easiest place to start is by making connections among the people and events that have shaped your life. Not only will you create a great story that others can read but you'll become a more creative self.

One of Aristotle's writings, *Poetics*, is widely regarded as setting the rules for poetry as it is known in Western civilization. Most of us might think that rhyming is what makes poetry special; however, this just isn't so. Aristotle wrote about the very heart of poetry in *Poetics* and noted, "The greatest thing by far is to be a master of metaphor." By this, Aristotle meant that metaphor and simile are at the heart of the poetic experience. They compare and connect things in phrases like "Life is like a river…" or "My love is like the ocean…"

Poetry fosters creativity because it makes connections and suggests relationships between things that might not be made through the more theory-driven process of scientific discovery. The theory-driven research process is a well-known and legitimate way to make connections between one thing and another. For example, research studies have mustered a great deal of evidence showing that diets high in fat can lead to heart disease and diets high in fiber lower the chances of colon cancer. The scientific process helps us establish a link between two previously unlinked phenomena.

Just like the theory-driven research process, poetry helps us establish a relationship between two previously unrelated objects—and Edison realized this. Instead of suggesting a link between a high-fiber diet and colon cancer, poetry suggests relationships between more abstract and random entities like life and rivers. Let's use an example from Edison's day that might be familiar to many Americans—Walt Whitman's poem "I Hear America Singing." In this poem, Whitman—arguably the greatest poet to document the American experience—compares the act of working to the act of singing. In doing so, he suggests that the best kind of work is something that fills us and makes us more human. Here's the poem so you can read the connection yourself:

I hear America singing, the varied carols I hear,
Those of mechanics, each one singing his as it should be blithe and strong,
The carpenter singing his as he measures his plank or beam,

The mason singing his as he makes ready for work, or leaves off work,
The boatman singing what belongs to him in his boat, the deckhand
singing on the steamboat deck,
The shoemaker singing as he sits on his bench, the hatter singing as he
stands,
The wood-cutter's song, the ploughboy's on his way in the morning, or
at noon intermission or at sundown,
The delicious singing of the mother, or of the young wife at work, or of
the girl sewing or washing,
Each singing what belongs to him or her and to none else,
The day what belongs to the day—at night the party of young fellows,
robust, friendly,
Singing with open mouths their strong melodious songs.

In this poem, Whitman surveys some of the most common jobs of Edison's early adulthood life—mechanic, carpenter, mason, boatman, and others—and suggests a connection between this independent kind of craft labor and the act of singing. The mechanized factory had already appeared on the American landscape and Whitman was careful to spotlight the craft-based jobs of the independent artisan or worker rather than the factory workers that were already starting to lose their song in the dehumanizing conditions of early industrialization.

Just over a century later, management researchers confirmed Whitman's connection between good work and good outcomes in a series of studies about job characteristics and work outcomes conducted by Richard Hackman and Greg Oldham. What Hackman and Oldham discovered was that workers find certain jobs more meaningful and satisfying than other jobs. They also found that workers were more motivated by jobs with more autonomy and more feedback. And that motivation and satisfaction increased when workers could complete meaningful and significant tasks entirely from start to finish rather than just being part of an assembly line. Is this an obvious conclusion?

Well…yes, but it's now an official conclusion validated by science. Walt Whitman suggested the same thing one hundred years earlier but used poetry rather than theory and data collection.

WHEN THE GOING GETS TOUGH, THE TOUGH WRITE POETRY

In 1911, an interviewer with *The Century* magazine asked Edison, "Do you think that our ideas have to be closely connected to our work to be useful?" Edison responded, "All kinds of ideas help to set the mind going. If a man has enough ideas to be an inventor, he can turn the same force in another direction, if he wishes to, and be a businessman, an architect, or anything." Maybe even a poet?

An increased rate of change has caused our world to become ever more fragmented and disconnected. Existing connections are either forgotten or shattered when new, disruptive technologies emerge. As such, the greater the rate of change, the more we need the creative connection maker. And the greater the opportunity for making connections, the more tools you need on your creative tool belt. One of Edison's most surprising tools for creativity was poetry.

Edison made connections between his inventions all the time. The phonograph was really just an offshoot—that is a metaphor—of the duplicating telegraph. The motion picture was connected to the phonograph. Regarding the motion picture, Edison said, "I want to do for the eye what the phonograph did for the ears." Robert Frost, one of America's best known poets, wrote, "There are many such things I have found myself saying about poetry, but the chiefest of these is that it is metaphor, saying one thing in terms of another." In other words, doing for the eye what the phonograph did for the ear.

Here's a poem by Edison. You'll notice that it consists of a number of fragmentary thoughts which he strings together into a connected whole. It may or may not work as poetry by literary standards, but it probably helped Edison keep making connections and, therefore, keep being creative.

A yellow oasis in hell—
Premeditated stupidity—
A phrenological idol
The somber dream of the gray-eyed Corsican
A brain so small that an animalcule went to view it with a compound
*   microscope*
The wrestling of shadows,
A square chunk of carrion with two green eyes
Held by threads of gossamer
Which float at midnight in bleak old rural graveyards.
Three million miles beyond the limits of the universe
Where the angels dare not go
There flies forever from nihil to nihil the foulest demon of the Cosmos.

Poetry helps us make sense of an increasingly fragmented world by allowing us to make connections between seemingly unrelated events or objects. Another great American inventor, Buckminster Fuller, stated, "All things, regardless of their dissimilarity, can be linked together either symbolically, physically, or psychologically." Go find the connections and use a poem if you have to.

E IS FOR EDISON

Key Lesson: Creativity is all about making connections.

- Where does it make sense in your company to rely on science and certainty? Where does it make sense to explore the unknown?
- Have you had a new experience in the last 30 days? How can you seek out a variety of career experiences to improve your intuition?
- What is the story of your company or my career? Write it down or tell it to another and look for connections that you may never have noticed.

PART II

INTERVIEW WITH AN INNOVATOR

"How to Succeed as an Inventor"

B Y 1898, EDISON WAS ONE OF THE MOST FAMOUS AMERICANS *on the planet and revered as the master inventor of the age. He had already invented the phonograph, electric light bulb, and kinetoscope—the forerunner to today's motion picture industry—and was hard at work trying to perfect an electric storage battery strong enough to power the newly invented automobile. People all over the nation were eager for him to share the secrets of his success and he responded with this essay that appeared in newspapers on April 3, 1898. Reproduced here exactly as it appeared, Edison shares advice on market demand, navigating the patent system, and his most basic success formula: sleep less and keep trying.*

If you want a recipe for how to succeed as an inventor I can give it to you in a very few words, and it will do for any other business in which you might wish to engage. First, find out if there is a real need for the thing which you want to invent. Then start in thinking about it. Get up at six o'clock the first morning and work until two o'clock the next morning. Keep on doing this until something in your line develops itself. If it don't do so pretty soon, you had better shorten your sleeping hours and work a little harder while you are awake. If you follow that rule, you can succeed as an inventor, or as anything else, for that matter. It was the following of just such a rule that led to the invention of the electric light, the phonograph and the kinetoscope.

I believe that any person, even of the most limited capacity, could become an inventor by sheer hard work. You can do almost anything if you keep at it long enough. Of course, the man with a natural aptitude would get there first, but the other plodder would eventually gain his point. The constant brooding on the one thing is sure to develop new ideas concerning it, and these, in their turn, suggest others, and soon the completed idea stands out before you. Above all things a man must not give up, once he has outlined his plan of action. A ball rolling down hill is sure to reach the bottom ultimately, no matter how many obstacles stand in the way. It is this principle which finally levels mountains. So, once fairly on your way, don't stop because of some seemingly impassable obstacle in front of you. What you want may be just beyond your nose, though you do not see it.

I once had that fact forcibly presented to me. I was working on an invention and finally reached a point when I could go no further. The thing lacked something but try as I might I could not tell what it was. Finally I got angry at it and threw the whole business out of the window. Afterward I thought how foolish the action was and I went out and gathered up the wreck. In putting it together again I saw just what was needed. Repairing the broken portions suggested it and it was so simple I wondered I had not seen it before. Now this little addition to the apparatus could have been ascertained by a little thoughtful experimentation. I suppose I found it out quicker because of the "accident" but that does not alter the moral of the incident.

How do I go about inventing a contrivance? Well, that is hard to say. Everything requires different treatment. First as I said, I find out if there is a real need for the thing. Then I go at it and attack it in every way I can think out. This multiplied attack soon simmers down, until I get what might be called a composite idea—something which is a combination of all I have thought before, or else the one feasible idea which really seems to discount all the rest. Having once got started on what I think is the right track I keep up the pace until the goal is reached.

The only thing, therefore, I can say for the young inventor is to go and do likewise. There is one piece of advice I can give, however. When a man starts in to invent let him do so with his mind free from all knowledge of what has been done already in the particular field he is investigating.

For instance, if I am about to work out something I never read up on it nor do I inquire what has been done on it by other inventors. Knowledge of this kind is almost certain to prove a snag in the path of the inventor. He gets into a rut made by his predecessors and stops off where they may have stopped. On the other hand, if he goes in a direction of his own, there are no ruts ahead of his: nothing in fact to obstruct his progress. I have several times made inventions in this manner: then when I had completed them I have read up on the subject. I found my own ideas were entirely original, but at the same time, the ideas of the other fellows were so good up to a certain point that I should have been tempted to have followed in their footsteps if I had done any previous reading up.

Of course the question of natural aptitude enters into the matter, and without it no man can become a star; nevertheless it is an auxiliary attainment: dogged perseverance is really the quality most to be desired. Dogged perseverance is the keystone of success. In the arts, such as painting, music, poetry, and so forth, a very special temperament may be required, but in the workshop of science men of the sanguine, "sandy" kind come out ahead. The man who keeps at one thing and never minds the clock is sure to do something. He may miss many social engagements, of course, but his success is assured.

What line of invention is most profitable? That depends on what is meant by the term "profitable." If an invention is of great public utility it is seldom personally profitable to the inventor. If, on the other hand, it is a money-maker for the inventor, then the benefit to the general public is apt to be limited. This is the fault of our modern patent office practice. Inventors are afraid to engage in large operations which would have to be protected by patents, for our laws as they now stand, give every opportunity to the sharks to go in and infringe the rights of the legitimate owners, employing eminent legal assistance meanwhile to cause a stay in any lawsuits instituted by the rightful inventor. I have inveighed against this condition before now. It is a serious discouragement to all great public inventions and it is a point which should be heeded by all who intend bringing out any invention.

So, then, as things stand, if a man wishes to make money from his inventions, he had better devise some little thing that costs but a trifle to manufacture. He will be sure to get fleeced if he does not. Then, when he brings the contrivance before the public, let him steer clear of the patent office, but manipulate the sale of his article so that no one can compete with him. His "trade secret" as it is called will be more valuable to him than any patent office papers, and it will cost him nothing to produce it.

After all, I suppose the real Simon Pure inventor is not apt to be a shrewd business man, and, therefore, the thing he wants to know principally is how to lay down any absolute rule. The history of great inventions shows that accident has been responsible for many initial ideas. This, however, is not always the case, nor should it be so. Given a small amount of aptitude and a large amount of application, any man can enter the business of inventing and make a living—scant at first, but more lucrative as he goes along. There are not many who realize what this "large amount of application" really means: the getting up very early, the staying up very late, and the sticking at it, meanwhile, with a vim that never can recognize failure. Men of this kind are sure to succeed.

Probably millions of persons are dabbling today in mechanical invention of some nature, but the most of it is too spasmodic to count for much in the long run. They do not keep at it enough. If a business man were to neglect the routine end of his daily work, if he were to go to his office one day or two in the week and then put the rest off until next Monday, or until some other time when the spirit moved him, he would soon have to resign. It is just so with invention. You have to pursue it as a business and even more steadily than the ordinary business.

EDISON AT HIS DESK IN THE LIBRARY OF THE WEST ORANGE LAB. THIS IS
WHERE HE CONDUCTED HIS ADMINISTRATIVE BUSINESS.

(Photo courtesy of U.S. Department of the Interior, National Park Service,
Edison National Historic Site)

Chapter 5

BUILD YOURSELF AN INVENTION FACTORY

T
HOMAS EDISON HAD TWO DESKS. AT LEAST THAT'S THE official story according to the virtual tour of the Edison National Historic Site in West Orange, New Jersey (www.nps.gov/edis/home.htm). If you tour the West Orange Lab in person or on the Web, you'll find one of Edison's two desks in the library in the main building. This desk is a classic rolltop with correspondence crammed into the dozens of cubbyholes at the back. It was at this desk that Edison received dignitaries (including presidents and other heads of state) and conducted business with the numerous executives that visited the West Orange lab from both his own and other companies.

The rolltop on the desk was pulled down and locked the day after Edison's death in 1931. The contents of the desk remained undisturbed for 16 years until 1947 when the desk was unlocked in celebration of what would have been Edison's 100th birthday. Today you can still see the contents of the desk exactly as Edison left them before his death.

His other "desk" is located in the chemistry lab. It isn't really a desk, however, regardless of what the pointer on the virtual tour might say. Rather, it's a workspace where Edison went to create rather than administrate.

Edison's two desks reflected his two sides: the inventor and the entrepreneur. Edison-as-inventor is symbolized by his

EDISON AT HIS WORKBENCH IN THE CHEMISTRY LAB AT
THE WEST ORANGE LAB. HE WOULD GO HERE TO
INVENT AND PLAY.
*(Photo courtesy of U.S. Department of the Interior, National
Park Service, Edison National Historic Site)*

workbench. Edison-as-entrepreneur is symbolized by his desk. Most of us would expect to find him experimenting at his workbench and this is indeed where he spent the majority of his time. However, he also ran a business. Both invention and entrepreneurship were important to his success but they require very different cultures.

So what's the big deal about a workbench? Well, most importantly, it's not a desk. Edison got his start working not behind a desk but behind a workbench. In contrast, most of us got our start working behind a desk—the great office relic of Corporate America. The desk-based culture of Corporate America and the workbench-based culture of Pre-Corporate America are two entirely different worlds. Edison and his colleagues went to the workbench to innovate and play with their new technologies. They rarely sat at a desk and shuffled papers.

Interestingly enough, much of this same culture is flourishing once again as America continues to transition into Post-Corporate America. This chapter will help you understand the work culture that surrounded Edison so you can better make the transition from Corporate America to Post-Corporate America. Innovation requires a culture very different from the one that now dominates Corporate America. The good news is that this culture can be recaptured with the help of a few basic ideas. When Edison wanted to get into the business of innovation on a full-time basis, he went and built himself an invention factory. The following might give you a few good ideas for doing the same.

INSULATED, BUT NOT ISOLATED

Almost every American is familiar with Henry David Thoreau's experiment in self-sufficiency at Walden Pond. Somewhere in either high school or college an English or political science teacher assigned Thoreau's book *Walden: Or Life In the Woods* for required reading. Let's admit it—It's invigorating to read how Thoreau intentionally left his comfortable urban surroundings and went off into the woods to build his own house, grow his own food, make his own furniture, and, well, just do everything for himself. Who among us does not get a secret thrill whenever we hear his line, "I went to the woods because I wished to live deliberately, to front only the essential facts of life, and see if I could not learn what it had to teach, and not, when I came to die, discover that I had not lived."

Like Thoreau, Edison exited the big city for the countryside in order to live more deliberately. In 1876, he left New York City and built his first laboratory in Menlo Park, New Jersey—25 miles away. There's one big difference between Edison and Thoreau, however. Thoreau's goal was to do everything for himself. Edison's goal was to do something for everybody else. He called

IN THE BEGINNING...

By now, it's clear that there are a lot of similarities between Thomas Edison and Silicon Valley. However, accounting records show that Edison was already doing business in Silicon Valley nearly a century before its transformation into the center of the Digital Age economy. Before Silicon Valley became Silicon Valley it was known as the Santa Clara Valley. In the mid-1800s, the Santa Clara Valley was populated primarily by ranchers and farmers although a surprisingly good mercury lode had been discovered too. In fact, the main newspaper for the region is still called *The San Jose Mercury News*.

In *The Big Score*, a history of Silicon Valley, author Michael Malone noted that Edison purchased $85,000 worth of mercury ore in the 1870s from mines in the Santa Clara Valley. Apparently, this mercury ore was for use in the development of the incandescent lamp. Regardless, Edison's economic blessing was already best owed on the humble valley and the Edison Electric Light Company returned later that decade to begin illuminating San Francisco and the surrounding region. From there it was a relatively short step from electricity to electronics.

A fellow named John Fleming modified an Edison light bulb with a metal plate and discovered that he could pick up high-frequency signals. This was the first step toward a working radio receiver. Lee De Forest, the father of American radio, later took Fleming's diode and added a third element that amplified the received signals. Thus was born the vacuum tube that served as the basic unit for the radio, and then television, and then the first computers until the invention of the integrated circuit in the 1960s.

his new laboratory at Menlo Park an "invention factory" and, in his own words, he planned to produce "a minor invention every ten days and a big thing every six months or so." Each and every one of these inventions would also have to be commercially viable—that is, something everybody uses.

Although there's a lot to like in Thoreau's story, there's also a lot to be concerned about from a business perspective. If everyone in America took Thoreau's advice and did everything for themselves, capitalism would crumble. Capitalism requires its participants to be *interdependent* rather than *independent* of one another. Edison's experiment did more to further capitalism than Thoreau's experiment because Edison "went to the woods" to create better products for future consumers.

Thomas Edison is credited with being the businessman who taught us how to separate the process of innovation from the process of manufacturing. There were a lot of factories in his day but they were all manufacturing factories. He established the first known "invention factory." His laboratory at Menlo Park was built specifically for the purpose of churning out as many inventions as possible. In fact, Edison came very close to establishing "invention quotas" similar to what we know as "manufacturing quotas."

Despite its physical separation, Edison's lab never became an ivory tower think tank that produced numerous but irrelevant or uneconomical ideas. To the contrary, the inventions that emerged from the laboratories in Menlo Park and later at West Orange have been some of the most practical inventions in the history of America. These two labs allowed him to be insulated but not isolated.

Edison chose Menlo Park as the site of his new laboratory for a couple of reasons. Obviously, it was a rural location and he had already learned the importance of solitude in helping him reach his creative peaks. However, Menlo Park was also located on the railroad and he and his boys could easily reach both Newark and New York City should business demand it. Chances are that his choice was influenced by the insulated world Edison experienced as a result of his deafness. Late in his life Edison penned a quote that neatly summed up his beliefs in this area: "The best thinking has been done in solitude. The worst has been done in turmoil."

A surprising number of America's most notable inventors and entrepreneurs grew up in the "middle of nowhere" far removed from the turmoil and congestion that can accompany urban living. One might think that the cultural and educational advantages associated with large cities would do more to form entrepreneurial talent than the quiet and boredom of the country. This just isn't always the case. Orville and Wilbur Wright, inventors of the airplane, not only grew up in the obscurity of the rural Midwest but they perfected their experimental aircraft on the remote shores of Kittyhawk, North Carolina. Oh yeah, neither of the Wright brothers had gone to college either.

The same holds for Edison. He spent his childhood in small towns in Ohio and Michigan. When he became a traveling telegrapher during his teens and early 20s, he lived the urban life in places like Memphis, Cincinnati, and Boston. In fact, much of his initial business success centered around opportunities in Boston and New York City. A funny thing happened when he decided to get serious about inventing—he went back to the solitude of the country. Edison didn't do this necessarily because he believed that there was something especially inspirational about nature. Rather, he deliberately moved to the country to separate himself and his work team for the process of invention.

So what did it look like? An interesting description of Edison's Menlo Park lab can be found in an 1878 issue of *Popular Science Monthly*. In it, writer G.M. Shaw described the second floor of the two-story Menlo Park lab: "The upper story occupies the length and breadth of the building, 100 by 25 feet, is lighted by windows on every side, and is occupied as a laboratory." Did you catch what's so amazing about that description? The lab was lighted not by electric light bulbs or gas but by sunlight! Edison invented the light bulb primarily by the light of the sun.

Today all of us are accustomed to the fact that there are some very large organizations out there with layers and layers of management and operations spanning the globe. This has not always been the case. Such organizations are barely over 100 years old. In fact, Edison's light bulb contributed to the growth of these multilayered companies because it allowed for the construction of larger buildings than ever before. The electric light bulb allowed architects the freedom to design large, well-lit, and windowless interior spaces for the first time. This one invention could easily double the size of most structures since gas and kerosene could not light these dark interior spaces nearly as well.

People would arrive at Menlo Park to find that it was neither a "park" nor the factory that they expected. Rather, it was a laboratory building and six houses. This lab seemed very different to the average visitor, and they often asked just what it was that was manufactured at Menlo Park. The answer, of course, was "nothing." It was the world's first invention factory.

HOW TO TELL IF YOU REALLY ARE WORKING FOR NAZIS

Have you ever heard (or said) the comment, "The managers here run this place like a bunch of Nazis!"? This kind of statement is usually uttered in response to some policy that restricts individual choice or creative freedoms. As bad as some workplaces are, even the worst are probably a long way from legitimate comparison to life under Nazi rule in the 1930s and 1940s.

The Nazis really did try to restrict the creativity of their subjects. Czecho-slovakian-born writer Josef Skvorecky recounts a set of their rules in his book *Talkin' Moscow Blues*. That book includes an essay called "Jazz" in which Skvorecky recounts an attempt by the German Nazis to keep their Aryan music free of subversive (i.e., creative) influences. In the thick of World War II, the Nazi authorities tried to crack down on the spread of jazz which they viewed as counterproductive to such Aryan ideals as conformity and order.

To aid in the crackdown, the Nazi authorities published a set of regulations to govern the playing of music in orchestras and bands inside German-occupied territories. These regulations allowed for creativity but only certain kinds of creativity and in certain percentages. Here are a few examples: Swing arrangements were limited to only 20 percent of the songs performed by orchestras or dance bands. "Hot jazz" and other "Negroid excesses in tempo" were strongly discouraged due to their non-Aryan nature characterized by "hysterical rhythmic reverses characteristic of the music of the barbarian races" (to quote directly from the Nazi regulations).

Certain instruments including cowbells, brushes, and saxophones were prohibited along with the use of mutes or hats to produce the dreaded "wa-wa" sound. Furthermore, the double (or stand-up) bass could not be played with the fingers—as is common in most jazz bands—but must be played using the bow. In addition, drum solos longer than a few seconds were prohibited along with any other form of vocal or instrumental improvisation.

In the end, the Nazi jazz regulations allowed for creativity but only a certain kind (if such a thing really exists). As we all know, the efforts of the Nazis failed and jazz rather than fascism triumphed in World War II. Furthermore, the creativity represented by jazz continues to outstrip the order and conformity demanded by fascism on every front—economic and otherwise. These regulations are the logical result of any effort to manage the creative process. You don't really manage creativity as much as you harness and focus its powers.

HARNESSING CREATIVITY WITH A FEW SIMPLE RULES

Edison realized that rules and regulations tended to hurt creativity, so he kept them as far from his labs as possible for as long as possible. One famous story involves a new worker showing up at Menlo Park (presumably fresh out of some factory setting in the Northeast) and asking where the rules for the laboratory were posted. The query must have offended Edison because he replied rather strongly with, "There ain't no rules here! We're trying to accomplish something!"

Machine-shop culture was characterized by its lack of rules. Edison seemed to have a disdain for posted rules, believing that they inhibited the flow of people, information, and creativity. Actually, Edison's lab did have rules of a sort; he just didn't have a long list of them posted, like many of the factories that existed in 19th century New England. I call his rules *cultural rules*. These type of rules are never posted on a wall but, rather, are coded into the genes of the firm.

Culture building is one of a manager's most important tasks. It's easy to see that different organizations have different cultures. Consider the cultural differences between two college football teams: Joe Paterno's Nittany Lions at Penn State and Bobby Bowden's Florida State Seminoles. Both coaches have won National Championships but did so by developing completely different cultures in their teams. Paterno's Penn State program is straight-laced and team oriented. It only draws attention to itself when it totally destroys an opponent. In contrast, Bowden's Florida State teams are rowdy, attention-getting, individual glorifying scoring machines. Both models work well, but both models are heavily influenced by the culture created by the two head coaches.

Businesses are no different when it comes to building culture. The culture will be affected by the implicit, invisible rules coded into the genes of the firm by its leaders. These are the cultural rules, and every manager needs to adopt a set to promote the outcomes most valued by the organization. If the organization's main goal is standardization, then the managers need to create a certain set of cultural rules. If the main goal is innovation, then the managers will need a very different set of cultural rules.

A current example of a highly innovative firm driven by a simple set of cultural rules is Miramax Films. You probably recognize Miramax from their film titles like *The English Patient*, *The Cider House Rules*, and *Shakespeare in Love*. Miramax has about four simple rules when it comes to filmmaking: you have to stay within a certain small budget, your film must tell a story, it must tell a story about a basic human need, and there must be a character with a personal flaw with which the audience can sympathize. Within these parameters, filmmakers are free to create any kind of film they wish and Miramax has experienced remarkable success over the past two decades. The company is widely credited for reviving the independent film, and its films are perennial favorites on the art house circuit.

As a manager, you can't just send out a company-wide e-mail titled "Creativity: Our Most Valued Activity" and expect people to be creative. Rather, you have to create a simple set of cultural rules that generate and reward creativity at every step of the process and at every level of the organization. E-mails (and their predecessor, memos) rarely change anything. Changing the cultural rules, however, will almost always change things.

Let's take a closer look at how Edison set up his invention factories because they don't look very much like the big companies that ruled Corporate America. His invention factories were open in both their design and information flows and very informal. Here are a few of the cultural rules that defined Edison's labs:

A revolving door. The work culture that dominated Edison's laboratories in the early days was rooted in the machine shops of 19th century America. A machine shop was a place where skilled craftsmen built from scratch the parts that ran the factories and businesses of the Northeast. Machine shops were characterized by a blend of raw capitalism and craft skills that both attracted highly skilled individuals and rewarded them for their accomplishments. The door to every machine shop worked both ways. It was always open and a person could walk in off the streets and begin working with only the most basic introduction. Likewise, a person—yes, even a talented one—was free to walk out and go elsewhere with only the most basic words of parting.

As strange as it may sound today, Edison allowed friends and visitors to conduct their own experiments in his well-appointed laboratory. All they had to do was pay for the supplies and labor they used. The lab was also open to any tramp mechanic who wished to make his home there for the time being.

A great deal of talent came through the door of Edison's labs. Some were invited to stay for the long term and some went back out the door and made their own mark in the history of invention. As discussed in Chapter 3, Edison often invited talented craftsmen to join his inner circle of inventors known as "the boys" but not everybody received such an invitation and some even left before they could be invited to stay. For example, another well-known electrical pioneer, Nikola Tesla, worked in Edison's labs for a short period before departing to make his own mark in the history of invention. Lesser known figures like Frank Sprague left Edison's lab in 1884 after a short stay and established the first electric street car system in America in 1887. Sprague's invention would go on to become a memorable symbol of urban living in the late 19th and early 20th centuries.

A problem-solving culture. One of the benefits of having a revolving door for talent is that you get numerous perspectives on your current problems. Since one of the most successful problem-solving techniques has been to approach the problem from as many new perspectives as possible, a revolving door increases the probability that this will occur. Some of our most long-standing problems have been solved quickly when outsiders look at the problem from a new perspective, and outsiders were always welcome in Edison's lab.

Everything about Edison's labs revolved around solving a problem and doing so quickly. He summed up his management philosophy once by saying, "in all laboratories like this one we have no system; we have no rules, but we have a big scrap heap." Bear in mind that Edison said this at the peak of the Scientific Management movement that prided itself on transforming factories by developing systems, imposing rules, and eliminating the waste of scrap heaps like Edison thrived on. He once told a government official that if he had a lab with a well-outfitted machine shop and experienced people working with him, "I could do almost anything in that shop…we can build anything, and build it quickly."

Edison's boasts about speed were not without merit. Prior to World War I, the world enjoyed an amazingly global economy with dependable supply chains for chemicals and commodities running between Europe and the

THE GLUE THAT HOLDS THINGS TOGETHER

In his book *Walt Disney: An American Original*, Bob Thomas recounts the story of how Disney described his job to a small child. By the 1950s, Disney had established himself as a successful producer of animated films and created a large company to handle their production. When a young boy asked Disney if he drew Mickey Mouse, Disney reluctantly admitted that he didn't draw anymore. The young man then asked Disney if he wrote all the funny lines for the features. Disney had to admit that he didn't do that, either.

Frustrated, the young boy demanded to know exactly what it was that the famous Walt Disney did. Disney replied, "Well, sometimes I think of myself as a little bee. I go from one area of the studio to another and gather pollen and sort of stimulate everybody. I guess that's the job I do."

Americas. When war broke out in Europe in the summer of 1914, these chains were suddenly shattered. Edison faced a shortage of carbolic acid that he had always purchased from England. Not only was it a key component in making his phonographic records, but it was also essential for making the explosives America might need should they have to enter the war effort.

According to an article in the *Bridgeport* [Connecticut] *Standard*, Edison and his team of workers

> ...spent three days and nights looking up and examining the different known processes of making synthetic carbolic acid. There are some half a dozen of them. He narrowed these down to one or two, took them into his laboratory and did some experimenting. Finally, at the end of the third day, he fixed on a certain one....He detailed 40 men, draftsmen

and chemists, and told them what he wanted; divided them into three eight-hour shifts, and gave the command to start. In a week, the plans were finished....Seventeen days afterward his plant delivered its first output of product, which other chemists assured him would take at least six months.

Far from six months, Edison managed to begin producing synthetic carbolic acid a mere 27 days after the war interrupted his supply. He was so hounded by other producers for some of his product that he built a second plant to meet the increasing demand as the war continued. Edison and company continued in the chemical manufacturing business for the next three years and constructed several more plants to produce a variety of essential chemicals previously obtained from German and English factories. By 1917, he decided to pull out of the chemical business but at no great loss to his pocketbook since he had designed the chemical plants to last only about three years.

An informal culture. It's arguable that Edison laid down the ground rules for the business casual attire that has dominated Post-Corporate America. In a 1913 interview with *Hearst's Magazine*, the reporter had this to say about Edison and his dress code: "Another Edison theory is that the clothing should be worn loose. Therefore, Edison never wears a collar that comes within half an inch of being as small as his neck. All his waistbands are large. Garters he will not wear at all because they pinch the arteries in the calves of his legs. His shoes are as big as his feet and then some. Except in the coldest winter weather, he wears low shoes. He never laces his shoes but once and that is when he buys them. He then laces them loosely. He says that nobody begins to know the amount of sickness and discomfort that are caused by tight shoes and tight clothing."

If anything characterized Corporate America, it was "tight shoes and tight clothing." For Edison, this type of clothing would only serve to constrict the flow of blood to the brain and other parts of the body. To him, a body under constant attack from its clothing is not a place where a brain can be most creative. Thus, he stayed loose and casual right down to wearing socks without garters (remember, these were the days before the invention of elastic).

Don't get too upset about this, either, but Thomas Edison had fun at work. All of the evidence indicates that he and his "boys" had a lot of fun with one another at his invention factories. Robert C. Halgrim, one of Edison's former workers, stated, "He was always playing practical jokes on everyone in the lab. You could pull one on him if you were good enough. It was his wonderful personality that kept one working for him, to realize that he was working harder than anyone else."

Edison knew that rules often ran counter to the goals of the innovation business. His rowdy, playful laboratories stood in stark contrast to the orderly, rule-driven factories that dotted the New England countryside. His labs were everything that the factories were not. In place of the discipline and order of the factory there was informality and messiness. Instead of efficiency there was waste—wasted time and wasted supplies. And then there was that pet bear they had for a while at the Menlo Park lab. You might be tempted to think that disorder was the key to Edison's success but that would be wrong. Underneath the disorder was the machine-shop culture discussed in Chapter 4. It was truly a "work hard—play hard" culture populated with results-oriented, professional craftsmen.

The craftsmen of Edison's day were serious about results but loved having fun. In fact, the work at the Menlo Park lab was constantly interrupted by practical jokes, games, and (believe it or not) sing-alongs at the pipe organ that occupied the back wall of the second-floor lab. All-night work sessions were often punctuated by a midnight feast with plenty of apple pie (a favorite of Edison's) and a couple of hours of storytelling before work resumed.

This kind of playful work culture seems as foreign to many of us as it did to some of the factory workers of Edison's day. We populate our office buildings with signs posted in the hallways that read "No Smoking," "Please Turn Out the Lights When You Leave," and "Open 9-5." One sign you'll never find in most businesses is the sign "Caution: Children at Play." There are a couple of good reasons that this sign is not around most office complexes. First, play was never an essential part of the culture of Corporate America that arose after Edison's heyday. Second, the idea of caution suggests that risk is accepted in your workplace. Play is risky because when you start playing, you never know where you're going to end up.

Edison's invention factories at Menlo Park and West Orange were fun places to work in more ways than one. Shortly after the invention of the motion picture, the world beat a path to Edison's laboratory door in West Orange to be immortalized in motion pictures. Being close to New York City had its advantages. A large number of Broadway's most popular acts came to the West Orange lab to be filmed at the makeshift studio they dubbed "The Black Maria" since it was covered on the outside with a dark tar paper. Making the early motion pictures was nothing short of a party. When the most renowned bodybuilder of his day, Eugene Sandow, came to the site to be filmed by Edison and his crew, the newspapers responded with headlines like "World's Strongest Man Meets World's Smartest Man." All the great vaudeville acts in New York City— dancers, bodybuilders, and acrobats—waived their usual fees and caught the train to West Orange to be put on film. Likewise, all the great musical acts came to make phonograph recordings. Even Buffalo Bill's Wild West Show featuring Annie Oakley traveled to West Orange to appear before the Edison cameras. The entertainment industry was being born and it was, well, entertaining.

WHERE'S YOUR LABORATORY?

In 1904, Edison was interviewed by a reporter from *Outing*, a recreation and outdoor magazine. "What do you do to keep your health?" the reporter inquired. "What are your recreations?" Edison responded without qualification, "Experimenting." Edison clearly loved experimentation. That is, he enjoyed trying things just to see what would happen.

Laboratory building may still be a legitimate path to success in Post-Corporate America. The good news is that if you have not yet built a

LISTEN WITH YOUR TEETH
Riding on Cowcatchers

In the summer of 1878, Thomas Edison traveled to the western United States with a group of scientists to observe a solar eclipse. Well…he traveled with them in the loosest sense of the term. The group of scientists went west on a Union Pacific train. Everybody except Edison rode in the coaches. Edison asked for—and received—permission to ride on the train's cowcatcher. You know, that steel grating that protrudes from the front of the train and knocks things off the track that would otherwise derail the locomotive.

Edison later described the events this way, "The engineers gave me a small cushion, and every day I rode in this manner from Omaha to [the] Sacramento Valley, except through the snowshed on the summit of the Sierras, without dust or anything else to obstruct the view." He took the same trip as everybody else but managed to see things from a different perspective.

Normality and routine are weak stimuli for creative thinking. A key step to becoming a more creative person is developing habits that help you see things from a different perspective—a non-routine perspective. Riding on the cowcatcher is all about learning how to get out of your routines. Take a different way to work tomorrow. Listen to music from another generation or, better yet, another country. Read a magazine you wouldn't usually read. Spend a day in the life of somebody else (try switching places with your most important customer). Eat food that scares you because it's so different. Most of all, GET OUT OF YOUR RUT!

laboratory, you can always build one into the existing organization. Experimentation involves risk-taking and that's why Edison is just as much an entrepreneur as he was an inventor. Both careers require a certain amount of risk-taking to succeed. Corporate America does not encourage risk-taking, although a few companies along the way have learned to incorporate it as an essential part of their identity in the transition to Post-Corporate America. One of these is General Electric.

General Electric has a bit of an unfair cultural advantage. The firm was originally known as Edison General Electric and was organized to exploit Edison's electrical patents. Of the original 12 members of the Dow Jones Industrial Average, only General Electric (GE) has survived to this day. During the 1980s, their now legendary CEO, Jack Welch, began a corporate-wide program of experimentation on a grand scale. Using this program, Welch did more to dismantle Corporate America than just about any other CEO in the past 20 years, although his efforts were sometimes misunderstood. When Welch started restructuring GE in the mid-eighties (half a dozen years before the downsizing craze swept the United States) he was vilified as "Neutron Jack"—a management weapon that got rid of people but left buildings intact. After two decades of constant transformation, GE is still considered to be one of the fittest of today's corporate giants.

What was Welch's secret? Laboratories. This should not come as too much of a surprise because, as I mentioned earlier, GE's corporate grandfather was Thomas Edison and it has a bit of the Old Man in its cultural genes. When Welch was asked about GE's success during a videotaped interview in 1994 with Professor Joseph L. Bower of the Harvard Business School, he explained the company's 12 strategic business units like this: "GE is 12 laboratories; each one competing in global markets; each one willing to transfer ideas that help the other one. Our job at the top is to take the ideas from one place and spread them to the others so we have the benefit of 12 labs for supply-chain management, working-capital management, or employee management."

Laboratories can take the form of businesses and they can also take the form of products. Have you heard of the film *Luxor Jr.*? How about *Tin Toy* or *Geri's Game*? No? Well, then maybe you've heard of the films *Toy Story, A Bug's Life, Toy Story 2,* and *Monsters, Inc.* You could hardly have missed the Disney/Pixar publicity blitzes surrounding these films. You've probably never heard of *Luxor Jr., Tin Toy,* or *Geri's Game* because these films were all in a category called "Animated Short Films" that are about five minutes long.

Pixar Animation Studios, the company behind *Toy Story,* has a laboratory mentality when it comes to creating great feature films. *Toy Story* became an instant classic upon its release in 1995. However, it didn't just spring out of nowhere. Rather, the technology that birthed *Toy Story*—computer-assisted animation—was cultivated in the laboratory of animated short films for almost a decade.

Pixar's first animated short about two playful desk lamps, *Luxor Jr.,* was released a full decade before *Toy Story* and received an Academy Award nomination in 1986 for Best Animated Short Film. Pixar went on to refine both their storytelling skills and their technological prowess and win the Oscar for Best Animated Short Film in 1988 with *Tin Toy* and in 1997 with *Geri's Game.* Pixar figured that if they could successfully make a technologically innovative five-minute animated short with memorable characters, then they could expand this model into larger, more successful feature films.

Dr. Edwin Catmull, Pixar's executive vice president and chief technical officer discussed Pixar's laboratory strategy this way in a recent press release: "Pixar sees immense value in preserving the short film as an art form and using it as a development tool for our creative and technical teams. The skills these professionals learn and polish are invaluable as we move toward our goal of creating one feature film a year." Has this business model performed well? Consider the evidence: *Toy Story* grossed $192 million during its domestic release in the United States, *A Bug's Life* ended it's run at $163 million, and *Toy Story 2* finished with a whopping $245 million.

THE POWER OF ONE

You should now have some understanding of the rich context of invention in which Edison lived and worked. It was undoubtedly an environment populated with talented people who shared information and challenged each other to constantly improve on the status quo. The myth that Edison was a lone inventor is just not true.

Edison's community of innovators gave him another advantage that his competitors simply lacked. The images of Edison working late into the night all by himself are simply false. Other inventors may have worked this way, but we'll never hear of them because they have slipped into the obscurity of history due to no results. The partnership at Edison's laboratories was so strong that it became harder and harder to separate what was one of his inventions from what was a group invention. This is especially true of his motion picture inventions. They were truly a group effort and would not have happened had it not been for the culture of innovation that Edison created around himself.

One of the key figures in the current attempt to create artificial intelligence is Nobel Laureate Herb Simon. Simon is a prolific idea generator with significant contributions in the fields of economics, psychology, sociology, and computer science. He stated, "The typical scientist is not a guy who doesn't show up at meetings. He participates. Science is not only the invention of ideas but the propagation of ideas." The point is not just to have ideas but to take these ideas and use them as the building blocks of other ideas. And yes, this is usually best done with a large group of informed people.

There's another myth that people often adopt in place of the "lone genius" myth. I call it the "teams are the answer" myth. The "teams are the answer" myth throws people into teams to solve every problem—regardless of either the problem or the people. The machine-shop culture of Edison's day did not promote teams for the sake of teams. Teams emerged naturally as mutually interdependent people grouped together to solve a common problem. The chemist needed the machinist and they both needed the engineer.

In the end, Edison mattered as an individual. He flourished in the invention factories he built in Menlo Park and West Orange. He would have been less without his "boys" but his "boys" would probably have been nothing without Edison. Great minds and great motives still matter. Edison's success was a matter of a great inventor placed in a great environment for invention. It wasn't just Menlo Park or West Orange and it wasn't just Edison—it was both...so please don't try to imitate it without an Edison.

E IS FOR EDISON

Key Lesson: If you want to invent, build yourself an invention factory.

- What would be the three most important institutional rules you would like to see at your company?
- How can you build these into your culture?
- Where can you create a laboratory in your company and start conducting dozens of small experiments?
- Who is the "Thomas Edison" within your company and what are you doing to keep him or her from going elsewhere?

Chapter 6

FAIL YOUR WAY TO SUCCESS

O NE OF THE MOST ENDURING MYTHS ABOUT EDISON IS that his life was a string of successful inventions. He did indeed have a number of very successful inventions and businesses. However, he also had many very expensive failures. The U.S. Patent and Trademark Office had granted Edison 1,093 patents at the time of his death. Let's call this the number of successful experiments. I've never put pencil to paper but I'd suspect that his total number of experiments could be as high as 100 times this many. Is that a 99 percent failure rate or a 1 percent success rate?

It's ironic that we use a light bulb to symbolize the flash of inspiration that comes with a new idea or solution. In reality, the invention of the light bulb was a long, slow process of trial and error. Whereas the phonograph came to Edison almost as a flash of inspiration, the light bulb took months of grueling work. If he had been judged by the standards of Corporate America during his efforts to invent the incandescent light bulb, he would have been fired. The invention was characterized by inefficiency, guess-work, waste, and failure after failure. It took several thousand trial-and-error experiments to find a successful filament for the incandescent bulb.

Edison and his boys started with metals both basic and exotic, including boron, nickel, molybdenum, chromium, and platinum. When carbon ultimately proved to be the highest probability material, Edison and his team settled on carbonized thread, that is, cotton thread cooked to a crisp in an oven. The choice was a success and the breakthrough carbon-filament bulb burned at least 13 hours, though legend has it the number of hours was upwards of 40. Once carbonized materials proved to be successful, Edison and his boys carbonized every combustible object they could lay their hands on including paper, fishing line, flax, coconut shell, human hair, and even bamboo hoping to find a filament that burned even longer. The irrepressible Edison would say at such times, "The trouble with other inventors is that they try a few things and quit. I never quit until I get what I want!"

Whereas the light bulb was a string of little failures that led to successes, Edison also experienced big failures that seemed to lead to nowhere but the loss of a great deal of money. Later in his life, Edison failed so horribly with an ill-fated mining venture that historians still call it "Edison's Folly" (more about this in the next chapter). Had the business venture succeeded, Edison may have been known primarily as an industrialist on the order of Rockefeller, Ford, and Carnegie. But it didn't, and Edison lost his fortune. Such a loss would have crushed lesser men but he had enough mettle and spirit to put the loss behind him and go forward to earn an even greater fortune in motion pictures.

WISDOM FROM THE RUNNER-UP

Charles F. Kettering is second only to Edison in the number of patents granted by the United States Patent Office. Not only did he invent the electric starter for automobiles, he also founded the Delco auto parts company and was head of research at General Motors for more than a quarter of a century. At the time of his death in 1958, Kettering arguably had impacted the automobile industry almost as much as Edison impacted the electric and entertainment industries.

Not surprisingly, Kettering was a great admirer of Edison and credited him with the idea of separating research and invention from all other activities.

Kettering was a popular commencement speaker, and one of his most oft-quoted speeches is an address he gave in 1940 called "Inventors and Inventions." In this speech, Kettering shared a remarkable perspective about failure:

> *An inventor is simply a person who doesn't take his education too seriously. You see, from the time a person is six years old until he graduates from college he has to take three or four examinations a year. If he flunks once, he is out. But an inventor is almost always failing. He tries and fails maybe a thousand times. If he succeeds once then he's in. These two things are diametrically opposite. We often say that the biggest job we have is to teach a newly hired employee how to fail intelligently. We have to train him to experiment over and over and to keep on trying and failing until he learns what will work.*

If you were to ask me the single most important paradigm shift you can make when it comes to creativity, I would refer you to Kettering's remarks. You simply have to learn to fail intelligently. It's critical to overcome the "one failure and you're out" paradigm and replace it with "one success and you're in." This doesn't mean you're playing the lottery every day at work when you invent. Innovation goes well beyond a game of luck. Innovation in the Edisonian sense is a game of ability in which you learn from your failure and profit handsomely from your successes.

In the bureaucratic organizations that ruled Corporate America, you were rewarded for avoiding failure. This is mainly because people were given orders from upper management that they were to follow almost without question. The biggest failure you could have in Corporate America was the failure to carry out the orders you were given. The marketplace that exists outside of every organization will not reward you for avoiding failure. At best, it will only tolerate you. To succeed in the marketplace in Post-Corporate America, you must not only be willing to fail, but to learn from your failures. As Kettering so aptly observed, if you succeed once, then you've done it and all the other failures will be viewed as stepping stones toward this success.

LISTEN WITH YOUR TEETH
Going for the High Numbers

Edison's failures teach us the benefits of considering later ideas as opposed to earlier ideas during the process of innovation. I conduct a traditional brainstorming exercise in my classes at Baylor University and try to accomplish several goals. First, I want the students to know that brainstorming is just one of many creativity techniques you can use to spur innovation. Second, and more important, I want the students to learn that you have to go through a surprisingly high number of bad ideas to get to a really good idea—and it helps if you're having fun at the same time.

At the beginning of the exercise, I give the student groups a clearly defined problem for which they need to generate solutions. Then I give the dreaded instruction: "OK, you'll have 20 minutes to brainstorm. Your goal is to develop 40 possible solutions in that period of time." The shock is audible as students gasp and moan. Nevertheless, they get going and often discover that they can generate upwards of 60 solutions when they really get cooking. I give them a few minutes to identify their most promising ideas and then choose the best to present to the class. I also give one additional instruction: I want them to tell the class what number this idea was in their list of 40 (or more) possible solutions.

The results are pretty predictable. Group after group stands up and says, "Number 34," "Number 27," "A cross between numbers 18 and 42." Up until that class, the students may have lived by the myth that creativity was having one great idea. The more accurate story is that creativity is having 30 bad but interrelated ideas that launch you to a great 31st idea. So don't just brainstorm. Brainstorm and go for the high numbers.

FORM FOLLOWS FUNCTION?

Louis Sullivan, the grandfather of architecture in America, built the first skyscraper to house the vertically charged organizations that arose along with Corporate America. Sullivan stated famously that "form follows function," meaning that the *form* that a building takes can be determined only after the *function* of the building has been determined. For example, if the function of a building is to provide a performance venue for an orchestra, then and only then can its appropriate form be determined. Likewise, if the function of a building is to serve as a shelter in a nuclear attack, then its form will be very different from that of a performance hall for an orchestra.

Harvard University professor Alfred DuPont Chandler, the grandfather of American business history, stated the business equivalent of Sullivan's dictum. Chandler studied the history and evolution of four of the most important corporations in American business: General Motors, The Standard Oil Company of New Jersey, Sears, Roebuck & Co., and DuPont Chemical Company. Chandler concluded from his study that "structure follows strategy," meaning that an organization must first have a clear vision of its competitive strategy before it can organize itself to achieve this strategy.

Both these dictums—"form follows function" and "structure follows strategy"—make common sense. Doesn't it stand to reason that a firm should wait to mobilize its resources until it has some idea of where it's headed? There's just one problem: Both of the above dictums are grounded in the assumptions that ruled Corporate America. This means that they're control and efficiency oriented and conservative enough to idolize standardization. Thankfully somebody has had the courage to challenge the two intellectual giants, Sullivan and Chandler. His name is Henry Petroski and he accomplished this feat by...well, by studying zippers, forks, and paper clips.

In 1992, Petroski, a civil engineering professor, published the book *The Evolution of Useful Things*. In it, he showed how a wide variety of common goods like zippers, forks, and paper clips came to their present form. His conclusions were very different than those of Sullivan and Chandler. In fact, Petroski concluded that "form follows failure," meaning that most of the useful items in our lives came about as innovative improvement on previously common products that were failing to meet our needs. For example, the paper clip was developed in response to the failure of ribbons, wax, and pins to adequately keep a stack of papers together. The unique form of the paper clip would not have come about were it not for the dissatisfaction people felt with the previous alternatives. In many ways, this was the story of the light bulb. Gas, kerosene, and candles were fine, but they failed on a number of counts, including safety. Edison built the light bulb on the shortcomings of the alternative forms of lighting.

Another good example of "form follows failure" is the invention of the donut. It is believed to have originated with a sea captain by the name of Hanson Gregory. Fried cakes were a popular treat in Gregory's day but they suffered from one major drawback: soggy centers. No matter how hot you got the oil, you just couldn't get the center part of a fried cake to cook. Not only was this unsavory, but the uncooked dough could also breed bacteria. Needless to say, this was very dissatisfying, but nobody noticed the opportunity for improvement.

Like others, Gregory accepted this shortcoming as destiny until a severe storm arose while he was at the helm. Needing both hands to steer, he shoved his fried cake over one of the spokes on the ship's wheel. Once through the squall, he realized that he had inadvertently removed the most unsavory part of the cake and could eat the remainder with pleasure. He ordered the ship's cook to begin frying cakes with holes cut in the center so as to allow a better distribution of hot oil to all parts of the dough. (A less dramatic version of this story suggests that Gregory simply told his mother to remove the center of the cake before cooking.) Some people would consider a smaller fried cake to be a failure. This isn't always the case, however. If the cake without the center is more pleasurable to eat, then less is more.

THE OINK STOPS HERE

Walt Disney's first great success story was a series of animated shorts called the "Silly Symphonies." The most successful of them all was the story of *The Three Little Pigs*. In it, Disney set to music the all-too-familiar story of the wolf and the pigs who built houses made of straw, sticks, and bricks. When it debuted in 1933, it became an overnight sensation and marquees all over the country billed the short cartoon above the main attraction with which it played. Most unexpectedly, the song from the film, "Who's Afraid of the Big Bad Wolf?," became a national rallying cry against the depression that was breaking the back of the United States.

Hoping to cash in on the film's popularity, the film's distributor, United Artists, pressed Disney and his people for other pig-related features. Walt Disney was initially resistant to the demand but was persuaded by his brother, Roy, to make three more pig-related sequels. None of the three sequels—*The Big Bad Wolf, Three Little Wolves,* and *The Practical Pig*—even came close to repeating the success of the original film. As a result, Walt uttered his immortal line: "You can't top pigs with pigs."

Others might have turned away, but Disney was smart enough to learn an important lesson from the failure of the three sequels. He learned that if you want to succeed in the entertainment business, you'd better avoid repeating yourself. Thankfully, he pushed the limits of creativity and brought forth such classic films as *Snow White and the Seven Dwarfs, Bambi,* and *Fantasia.* Disney's commitment to originality and willingness to learn from failure is a role model for innovators in every industry.

Even though it's only three words, the idea that "form follows failure" has vast implications for those who want to manage the process of innovation. "Form follows function" results in the proverbial analysis paralysis that tempts you to have all the answers before you start acting. There's certainly something to reflection, but Corporate Americans reflected so much that they often missed out on opportunities pursued by the less reflective and failure-loving Edisonian types of Post-Corporate America. If nothing else, "form follows failure" results in a bias for action. It's a ready-fire-aim kind of approach that paid great dividends for Edison. Also, "form follows failure" relies on dissatisfaction with current alternatives. Maybe the easiest way to create the next great technology is to look for sources of dissatisfaction in everybody's life and develop new alternatives. If you need some inspiration, most of us don't like getting shots at the doctor.

FAILURE AS UNEXPECTED OUTCOMES

To create a culture that tolerates failure, it might be helpful to redefine failure. One way is to recognize that while it can create dissatisfaction, it can also motivate us toward greater successes. And it can lead to unexpected outcomes. That is, when you expect one thing and get another, you might consider that a failure. However, this is not always a bad thing because your unexpected result can be something wonderful.

One example of this type of failure is best captured in the invention of the chocolate chip cookie. Ruth Wakefield invented this all-American staple in 1930 at the Toll House Inn near Boston. She was making a batch of chocolate cookies when she discovered she had run out of baker's chocolate. To solve this problem, she broke off pieces of a semisweet chocolate chunk and dropped them into the batter. She expected the pieces to melt while the cookies baked and turn the plain dough cookies into ones that were brown and chocolaty through and through. She discovered, however, that the chocolate didn't melt and she had inadvertently invented the chocolate chip cookie—an American classic.

WHEN RANDOM IS OK

Fostering creativity is one of the few times that it's good to be random. The next time you need to spur creativity in a meeting or problem-solving session try one of these random tactics:

Random Response. This creativity-enhancing activity is like taking one of those ink blot tests. Let's say you're in charge of planning the social activities for your next professional meeting and you'd like to get beyond the safe, traditional habit of wine-and-cheese mixers every evening. Try bringing a box to your next program planning meeting with six random objects inside (let's say a candle, an old 45-rpm record, a picture of Jim Carrey, a pineapple, a Canadian flag, and a toy flying saucer). Pass out sheets of paper to the planning committee with the numbers one through six and give the following instruction: "Inside this box, I have six items. As I pull out each item, write down whatever program ideas come to mind as a result of seeing this object." Next, pull out the items and coach the group into recording all of their ideas. Finally, go around the table and see what you've created. Chances are, somebody is going to have started thinking in a new direction just because of the random jolt that you gave them.

Random Items. If you're alone, you can use randomness to spur your creativity, too. Next time you're brainstorming and get stuck, try looking at the 12th advertisement in the nearest magazine that you can find or pull down the dictionary and look at the 18th word on page 357 to see if it sends you in any new directions. If these don't work just switch the numbers and try again.

Some people might argue that Ruth Wakefield was the "luckiest person alive." However, her story doesn't fit my definition of luck. She should be applauded for putting these "faulty" cookies up for sale anyway. When she did, her customers voted with their money and signaled to her that this "failure" wasn't a failure after all. Ruth Wakefield simply expected to do one thing that everybody wanted and ended up doing another thing that everybody wanted even more. Therefore, it might be a good idea to put your next failure up for sale anyway because somebody might think it's a good idea.

Some of the greatest business success stories involve complete surprise. It's not that these businesspeople just stumbled across a great business idea. Rather they stumbled across a great business idea *while doing something or going somewhere else.* Edison often relied on unexpected outcomes to lead him in a new creative direction. In an interview in the January 1921 *American Magazine,* Edison had this to say about failure:

> *You see, in trying to perfect a thing I sometimes run straight up against a granite wall 100 feet high. If after trying and trying and trying again, I can't get over it, I turn to something else. Then some day, it may be months or it may be years later, something is discovered either by myself or someone else, or something happens in some part of the world, which I recognize may help me to scale at least part of that wall.*
>
> *I never allow myself to become discouraged under any circumstances. I recall that after we had conducted thousands of experiments on a certain project without solving the problem, one of my associates, after we had conducted the crowning experiment and it had proved a failure, expressed discouragement and disgust over our having failed 'to find out anything.' I cheerily assured him that we had learned something. For we had learned for a certainty that the thing couldn't be done that way, and that we would have to try some other way. We sometimes learn a lot from our failures if we have put into the effort the best thought and work we are capable of.*

I've concluded that Edison avoided the discouragement that often accompanies failure by having a sense of delight about life. He was known to dance around his lab when some unexpected result sent him in an unforeseen direction. Delight may be the greatest casualty from the reign of Corporate America. In fact, the entire era was symbolized by the term "The Man in the Grey Flannel Suit." The opposite of a sense of delight is the attitude of "no surprises, please." It's a reactionary stance that considers all unexpected outcomes unpleasant because…well, because the unexpected is just unpleasant.

Having a sense of delight is so easy that even a three-year-old child can do it. A three-year-old child is full of delight and displays this attitude with such phrases as "Mommy! Did you see that (a) bug, (b) car, (c) animal, (d) toy? I've never seen a (a) bug, (b) car, (c) animal, (d) toy like that before!" Contrast that with what your predictability-loving supervisor from Corporate America might have said: "Johnson! Is this your (a) idea, (b) tie, (c) report, (d) office? We've never seen a (a) idea, (b) tie, (c) report, (d) office like that before…and we'd better not see it again!" The difference is clear. Children tend to embrace the unexpected with delight whereas control-oriented managers tend to react to it as deviant. I guess we could say that Edison was childish from time to time. He seemed to grow more and more excited with each failure as it seemed to be a step closer to the elusive solution.

GUIDELINES FOR FAILING INTELLIGENTLY

In my previous book, *Ben Franklin's 12 Rules of Management,* I argued that one of the most important factors to have on your annual performance review is "Number of Successful Failures." A successful failure is one that provides you with feedback so rich that it results in a new business opportunity. In an all-out effort to take my own advice, this past year I added an interesting new component to my college classes: documented failures. I teach a negotiation class at my university and all students in the class now are required to provide evidence of failure in a variety of negotiations throughout the semester.

THE INCREDIBLE GROWING BRAIN

Legendary New York City teacher John Taylor Gatto was recently asked in an interview how to best unlock the genius residing in most students. He replied, "When the mind is tested against something unfamiliar, it grows in front of your eyes." Gatto cited research documenting that adopted children tend on average to score 20 points higher on standard IQ tests than the siblings from their original biological families. Researchers believe that much of this is due to the reality of constantly having to navigate a newer and stranger environment than their biological siblings. Learning theorist Roger Schank echoes this belief by stating that "expectation failure" is the foundation of learning. By this he means that you expected one thing, got another, and your mind starts working to solve the discrepancy.

When I added the component to the class, I quickly realized that my students were either afraid of failure or had forgotten how to fail altogether. Upon learning of the course requirement, a common student response was to share with me some story from the past year or two and invariably it would end with something like, "…it was sooooo embarrassing. Does this count as a failure?" A couple of things fall out of this comment. First, students seem to define failure as "personal humiliation" rather than the opportunity for a positive learning experience. Second, they are asking if their failure meets my standards. That is, they are assuming that any failure will be punished so they had better clear it with their "supervisor" first. The bottom line is that they have been socialized to avoid failure.

I've learned that the forces of Corporate America are against me. The school system—even at the university level—has trained my students to make "A's" at all costs and that usually means taking somebody else's orders and avoiding failure, or "F's." As a result of this, I've had to coach my students on "how to fail intelligently" to use Charles Kettering's phrase. You would think that failure ought to be the easiest thing in the world for a college student but it's actually proven to be quite challenging. Since many of my college students will become your employees, I thought it might be useful to share with you how I'm coaching them to learn from failure. Below are some guidelines for teaching your workers to fail intelligently.

Have a plan for success. Learning theorist Roger Schank argues that expectation failure is central to the learning experience. That is, when you expect one thing and you get another, you have an opportunity to learn. Phrases like "I never expected this kind of resistance," or "I never realized that the market could be so big," suggest that the stage is set for learning. Thus, the first step in failing intelligently is to have some kind of expectation. I therefore challenge my students to enter their negotiation assignment with a plan for success: "I want to make $50,000 per year," or "I want 30 percent off the listed price."

Edison was able to learn from his failures precisely because he learned to recognize such expectation failures when they occurred. Sometimes his failure just eliminated another possibility in a long line of experiments, such as during his search for a workable filament for the electric light bulb. Other times, he expected one result and got another, like when the repeating telegraph led to the invention of the phonograph.

Reflection and change. A second key to failing intelligently is reflecting on your failures and changing your behaviors. Believe it or not, this is actually called learning, but most of us wouldn't recognize it as such. Our traditional education has socialized us to believe that learning occurs when we stuff a number of formulas and definitions into our heads just long enough to give them back on an exam. Although new information can promote learning, the clearest evidence of having learned is a change in behavior.

In my negotiations class, I require my students to reflect on their failures by writing about them. I ask them to answer such questions as "What caused the negotiation to fail?" This challenges students to reflect on the failure and make a preliminary diagnosis of what went wrong. The final question for the documented failures in my class is "What could you do next time to avoid the same kind of failure?" Answering this starts the process of experimentation all over again by developing a new expectation or "plan for success." Put differently, it sets up a feedback loop in a process of constant experimentation.

A DIFFERENT KIND OF M&M

Corporate America made failure fatal, but steps can be taken to build failure back into your organization. One possible solution for building failure back into Post-Corporate America is to institutionalize failure. Institutionalizing failure means that you learn to accept it as part of life and you set up simple rules and institutions within your organization for learning from failure without getting fired.

In spite of its rather glamorous treatment in television dramas like *ER* or *M*A*S*H*, the life of a surgeon is one that looks death in the face on an almost daily basis. Surgeons are even known to make mistakes, from highly-publicized errors like sewing a surgical instrument inside a patient's abdomen to less dramatic ones like prescribing the wrong medication.

Both surgeons and the public they serve are well aware of the mistakes that can happen. By and large, the public has responded with the only weapon available to them: lawsuits. Unfortunately, lawsuits force the physician and patient into an adversarial relationship that punishes failure. In extreme cases, the patient might get a handsome payout, but researchers have shown that legal actions and the hefty settlements that accompany them are doing little to change the number of physician mistakes.

Fortunately, physicians have developed their own response to reducing the number of mistakes made during surgery and it's called the Morbidity and Mortality Conference (M&M for short). Every week, surgeons in hospitals all over the nation gather together to have a frank and professional discussion about the errors—however minor—that have occurred at the hospital. Sometimes it can be something as minor as prescribing too little medication. Other times, it can be something major like amputating the wrong limb. Regardless, each error is brought before the group, discussed by the attending physician, carefully analyzed, and then critiqued with the question, "What would you have done differently?"

The M&M conference is a model for how to handle failure in a professional, productive manner. Everybody in the room realizes that each failure presented before the conference has an associated cost that is paid in human suffering. Whereas most of us would shrink from such a confrontation, the culture of the conference is one that encourages personal accountability and continual learning. Amazingly enough, all of this is accomplished in an environment free of legal and professional penalty. The M&M conference realizes that errors are a part of the medical process, but also suggests that they are still an intolerable part. In this same spirit Thomas Edison once said, "What is a college? An institute of learning. What is a business? An institute of learning. Life, itself, is an institute of learning."

E IS FOR EDISON

Key Lesson: The greatest innovators have made a lot of F's.

- How does your company handle failure? Is it punished immediately, tolerated, or rewarded?
- What can you do to promote successful failures within your firm? Is it possible to build it in as a performance measure?
- Is there a forum within your company (like an M&M) where failures can be diagnosed and discussed in a professional atmosphere?

Chapter 7

MR. EDISON GOES
TO WALL STREET

HE 1920S WERE CALLED THE "ROARING 20S" AND THAT roar echoed down Wall Street. In a single decade, the Dow Jones Industrial Average increased an unprecedented 500 percent. The Dow was driven by a variety of new technologies that were changing the lifestyle of every home and business in America. Sounds kind of like the '90s, huh? One man got most of credit for the market boom and that man was Thomas Edison. In fact, in 1923 the *New York Times* estimated that over $15 billion dollars were invested in industries either started or heavily influenced by Edison—a significant portion the money invested in the entire stock market at that time.

When it comes to negotiating with capitalists, it often takes three or four people to bring the same talent to the table that Edison brought by himself. Venture capitalists are accustomed to seeing a management team with a marketing type, a technology type, a management type, and a brand-name figurehead. Edison was all these and then some. He was a complete package that could invent, manage, and promote at the same time. The Edison brand was so firmly established in the marketplace that an investment in it was like money in the bank for a capitalist.

This chapter will try to help you understand the critical role that venture capital has always played in America and to show you how Edison was able to attract the lion's share of capital in

---

his day. Not only was he a master of making creative connections at the work-bench but he also connected himself to venture capital networks and publicity networks (more on this in Chapter 8). It will also discuss some of his short-comings as a businessman. He might have been an attractive investment but he wasn't perfect. Hopefully, you will be able to build on his successes and learn from his mistakes.

IS BUSINESS THE BAD GUY?

Considering what they've done to build this country, American history does not treat its businesspeople very well. This is true both for business man-agers and the capitalists who provide them with money. You've probably heard the phrase "robber barons" associated with famous businessmen like John D. Rockefeller. Historian Matthew Josephson popularized that phrase in his 1934 book by the same name. Josephson is also one of Edison's first and most respected biographers. Nevertheless, his biography of Edison smacks of an antibusiness bias. For example, the chapter in which he discusses Edison's dealings with Wall Street is called "The Inventor and the Barons." This is clearly a good guy/bad guy title. The good guy? The "inventor," of course. Josephson effectively strips Edison of any semblance of business by drawing him as an inventor rather than the entrepreneur he rightfully was. And the bad guy? That's the "robber barons" on Wall Street. Edison was more than an inventor, he was an entrepreneur. And the barons were not robber barons, they were venture capitalists.

Josephson's titles reflect a long-standing assumption that business is the bad guy. Hollywood has gone a long way in promoting this myth with bad guy capitalists in films ranging from Oliver Stone's *Wall Street* to *Other People's Money* to, more recently, *Titanic*. You mean, the billion-dollar-my-heart-will-go-on *Titanic*? Absolutely. The biggest schmuck on the boat was an American industrialist. It was no different 60 years ago when they made movies about Edison's life.

If all you know about Edison is from the 1940 movie *Edison, the Man* starring Spencer Tracy, then you're missing a great deal of the real story. Every film needs a good villain and it certainly was not going to be the much-admired Edison—even if he had been dead for almost a decade. In his day, he was revered as highly as George Washington or Abraham Lincoln. Since he was out, Hollywood decided to find its villain on Wall Street in the form of a dirty-dealing capitalist named Taggart.

In the film, Edison outwits any capitalist he meets when negotiating the price for his inventions. He is also portrayed as more inventor than business-man and the film deliberately showcases how he lets his bills stack up and costs go unchecked. He somehow avoids raising any capital throughout the movie. That is, he manages to finance his own operations by mysteriously selling his inventions without the slightest bit of working capital to keep him going. Worst of all, the capitalist Taggart is portrayed in the film as trying to set Edison up for failure as Edison works to electrify New York City. Taggart apparently holds a large number of gas stocks whose value would plummet should Edison's electric lighting system work. The capitalist Taggart therefore tries to thwart the inventor Edison at every juncture, but we all know that Edison will triumph in the end.

In one pivotal scene, Edison is at wit's end in his quest to invent the incandescent light bulb. He wanders into Taggart's offices on Wall Street in hopes of getting some funds so he can pay his men and keep his Menlo Park invention factory running. Taggart agrees to float Edison a surprisingly large amount of capital in exchange for creative control over his inventions. At the last moment Edison turns down the offer and thwarts the dastardly Taggart's plan to shut down his electrical progress.

Thankfully, the film is more fantasy than reality. Edison may not have been a model accountant but he was surprisingly good at raising capital in a capital market that was hostile and primitive by today's standards. He did so with some of the biggest names in the business: the Vanderbilt family, J.P. Morgan, Henry Villard, and Jay Gould. In fact, Edison's Wall Street savvy probably gave him a competitive edge over many of the other inventors of his day. Sure, there were some capitalists with large holdings in gas stocks that were eager to see Edison fail in his quest for electric light. However, there were just as many eager to see Edison succeed and gladly provided him with seed capital. That's how the system works.

IN DEFENSE OF VENTURE CAPITALISTS

OK, so you don't call them venture capitalists but "vulture" capitalists. Maybe you've had some bad experiences with venture capitalists (VCs) in the past. You know, things went well that first round of funding but now you need more money and they're willing to give you more in exchange for majority

ON NOVELTY AND NECESSITY

As Edison began to revolutionize the way people illuminated their homes and offices he stated, "We will make electricity so cheap that only the rich will burn candles." Such prophetic sayings lend credibility to the notion that Edison also founded the modern candle industry populated by such well-known retailers and brands as Wicks-N-Sticks, The Yankee Candle Company, and the A.I. Root Company. Every time a newly wedded couple gets a set of candlesticks, Edison's prophetic words ring true once again.

His business sense on this issue is worth taking note of. Edison realized that a good deal of business opportunity lay in creating better solutions for problems such as illumination. That's obvious, so where's the wisdom? He also points to market opportunity that exists whenever a product, like candles, is made obsolete. He realized that the price of candles would rise as the demand for candles control in the company. Now you feel like they deliberately undercapitalized you so they could gain control with a second round of funds. For you, it's all downside and little upside. For them, it's all upside and absolutely no downside—or so it seems. Things started out well and it seemed like the VC was always there for you as calm and helpful as Flipper, the dolphin. Now, things are going poorly and you can never get on their calendar when you really need it. They're starting to look less like Flipper and more like a shark.

Well, if they are sharks then they are our sharks. By "our sharks" I mean that they are America's sharks. Venture capital is one of the things that has made America unique as an economic power. It is one of the main reasons the United States of America has enjoyed such tremendous economic growth for the past two decades. Unlike their more conservative investment banking

decreased. Thus, there's money to be made in obsolescence. The candle industry went one further and created candles that were valued not for their illumination abilities but for their scent and design. The average American from the late 19th century would faint were they asked to pay the $20-something price for a Yankee Candle—especially when this price is adjusted for inflation.

Remember this: today's obsolete product is tomorrow's emergent business opportunity. Who's out there looking for new ways to exploit technologies that are on the cusp of obsolescence like film-based photography, the internal combustion engine, or the personal computer? I'm just guessing on this list but you could probably find a futurist somewhere who could make a serious argument that these technologies might have already reached their peak. As fuel cells loom on the horizon, it's already becoming fashionable to leave a wedding ceremony in a classic 1950s gas-guzzling convertible.

counterparts, VCs were willing to take some big risks on unknown companies like Apple Computer, SUN Microsystems, and Cisco Systems—the companies that formed the backbone of the Digital Revolution. Love them or hate them, VCs have more often than not been the catalyst that sparked America's economic growth. If I were to sum up why we won the Cold War, it would be this: We had capitalists. They had bureaucrats.

Why is it that some countries, like America, are constantly changing while other countries seem to stagnate like "The Land That Time Forgot?" The answer is that a capitalist nation like America has a built-in system to reward change, whereas countries run by bureaucrats resist change. Bureaucrats don't want change because it does not reward them. They find the status quo very lucrative. VCs, on the other hand, find change rewarding if they invest in the correct emerging opportunities. In the movie *Edison, the Man*, the bad-guy capitalists all held huge positions in gas stocks that would lose a great deal of their value should Edison's electrical inventions work. They opposed Edison at every move but the heroic inventor ultimately triumphed in a victory of the common man over the capitalist. In reality, investors were lining up to provide Edison with funds to perfect his electrical inventions. It's not too much of an exaggeration to say that were it not for venture capital, Edison's electrical revolution may never have happened and you might be reading this book by gas lamp instead of electric lamp.

VCs have helped create the only country on earth where failure isn't fatal. Failure is OK in the United States and this just isn't true in every culture. There are few negative repercussions from trying a new enterprise and failing in the United States. In fact, people who do are often welcomed back into the corporations they left and considered a bit wiser for the experience. Your risk rating may go up next time around if you fail too often, but that doesn't mean people will be unwilling to invest in you and your ideas—it just means they'll charge more.

When working with VCs, keep two things in mind that will help you understand the world from their perspective. First, they run the closest thing to a genuine meritocracy on the planet. By meritocracy I mean that capital flows to the most deserving recipient regardless of gender, race, color, creed, age, or national origin. VCs are motivated to make deals and if you've got the goods, you'll eventually get funded. A second thing to remember is that most people, including VCs, are both risk averse and loss averse, meaning that they would favor a certain gain rather than take a gamble. Most VCs will model the dual characteristics of risk aversion and loss aversion when structuring their deals. That is, they will most likely structure their deal to give themselves an unlimited upside coupled with the strongest downside protection they can find. Like it or not, this helps them manage their risk and make more deals each year.

HOW EDISON GOT (AND KEPT) THE CAPITAL FLOWING

Edison's ability to attract a steady stream of capital was central to his success as an inventor. He was better at attracting capital than were the dozens of other inventors hoping to be the first to invent the incandescent light bulb. He didn't necessarily like working with VCs either, but recognized them as a necessary part of the process of invention. So why was he so successful at attracting capital? Here's what a careful study of Edison's life suggests.

You can attract more capital with a good reputation. When he began his work on the incandescent light bulb, Edison was already a national celebrity as a result of inventing the phonograph. Prior to the invention of the phonograph, he was well known on Wall Street for his telegraph-related inventions, like the quadruplex telegraph and stock tickers that allowed investors to monitor markets almost instantaneously. Edison's name was out on the street, and not just any old street, but Wall Street.

Edison recognized the value of his name and used it to attract capital. In fact, he had no track record whatsoever in electric lighting systems when he began his work on the incandescent bulb. His successes up to that point had been primarily in the telegraph and phonograph. He deliberately chose to pursue the incandescent light bulb because he saw an emergent opportunity. It's clear that he used the Edison name, more than a pattern of successful experiments in electric lighting systems, to attract capital.

Bet your reputation with a big promise. In September 1878—a full year before Edison created a working model of the incandescent light bulb, he announced a "big bonanza" to a reporter with the *New York Sun.* It was almost as though P.T. Barnum were acting as his press secretary. In a series of interviews with the *New York Sun, New York Herald,* and *New York Tribune,* Edison announced that he had not only obtained an electric light bulb from an entirely different process than other inventors had used, but that he expected it could produce "...a thousand—aye, ten thousand lights from one machine."

Not only did he suggest that he had come upon the secret of electric illumination, but he also boasted that he would light up the entire area of downtown New York with 500,000 incandescent lamps powered by a handful of steam dynamos. This was a big promise and it took Edison over a year to deliver a working light bulb and even longer to successfully wire lower Manhattan. Keep in mind that anybody can make a big promise in order to attract the attention of investors. However, savvy investors aren't going to listen to your "next sure thing" because experience has taught them that most sure things are just another empty set of promises. Edison could make a big promise and attract a great deal of capital because he had an established reputation (or record of success) to back it up.

Keep the wolves at bay with small victories and regular reports. The common myth is that Edison electrified the world. The reality is that he electrified only a very small part of it. He didn't start by wiring the world for electricity. Rather, he started out by wiring his Menlo Park laboratory with electricity and letting New York City come out to view the spectacle. Next, he took the spectacle to New York City with the installation of the Pearl Street electrical station that powered the lower part of Manhattan. These were very small and early wins that were important in establishing his reputation as the technology leader in the emergent electric industry.

Strategy consultant Gary Hamel calls this the "win small, win early, win often" approach. Despite his fame surrounding his electrical inventions, Edison had only these two small victories associated with his electric lighting inventions. Given that everyone and everything plugs into a wall socket these days, his two small victories look rather miniscule in retrospect. But the difference between zero and one is greater than the difference between any other two numbers. It is the difference between nothing and anything. Small wins are big wins when the next best alternative is nothing.

I mentioned that over a year passed between the time of Edison's initial announcements and funding and his creation of a working light bulb. As the months dragged on, Edison needed more than big promises to keep the capital flowing. To keep the anxious shareholders happy, he gave regular reports and often invited them out to the Menlo Park lab for lavish dinners and prototype demonstrations. He did the same for New York City bureaucrats who had to be carefully courted to give him permission to wire lower Manhattan for electricity. Edison understood that a little information is better than no information and that a good working relationship could help overcome resistance.

Invent a system, sell a product. Some inventors create new products, but Edison often created entire systems. Before he could invent the electric light bulb he had to invent a working electrical system. (Remember that the lab where the light bulb was invented was illuminated by gas lamps.) One characteristic that set Edison apart from all of the other inventors trying to be the first to create an electric light bulb was his ability to think clearly at the system level. When he sought capital for his light bulb project, VCs could see that it was just one small part of a much larger undertaking.

IN PRAISE OF WEAK LINKS

You may have heard the phrase, "A chain is only as strong as its weakest link." As with most bits of traditional wisdom, it's only partly right. Edison had a different view of weak links. In fact, he sort of invented the "weak link" but called it the "safety-catch." Today, we call it the fuse.

The fuse was invented as part of Edison's original Pearl Street power station installment and became standard in all electrical installations thereafter. Fire safety was probably the number-one marketing concern associated with the installation of electricity and Edison had to find a way to minimize this concern as much as possible. The fuse was his answer and his goal was to signal to the buyer that the electrical system they were about to purchase was literally "foolproof." That is, an Edison system had built-in protection against inexperienced operators. Should a child or an uninformed employee accidentally send too much electrical power through the home or business system, the fuse would break and save not only the electrical system but the home or business as well.

Edison's clever use of the weak link should challenge us to rethink our position regarding the role of weaknesses in systems. From his perspective, weak links were essential. After all, which would you rather lose: the $30,000 system or the 3¢ part? That's not a hard question. Think of it as the "canary in the coal mine." Coal miners used to carry canaries with them down into the mines as a weak link. Canaries were more fragile than humans and would succumb to noxious gases more quickly. If the canary died, the humans would be next—even if they didn't feel in danger at the time. In this example, the weak link was part of an early warning system.

The phrase "killer app" was coined in the '80s to refer to the "killer" or "must have" computer software applications that pulled more expensive systems into new markets. The spreadsheet was the killer app for the personal computer. Desktop publishing was the killer app for the Macintosh computer. E-mail was the killer app for the Internet. Likewise, the electric light bulb was the killer app that made the installation of electrical systems in neighborhoods all over the United States a consumer imperative.

Edison understood this point and never talked about inventing electrical systems. He knew this would be a rather dull idea to try to sell to the press and to capitalists. Electrical systems were also invisible since they were buried underground, inside walls, or strung out of sight above people's heads. So Edison focused everybody's attention on the visible and exciting possibility of a working electric light bulb. Of course, an entire system of generators, wiring, lamps, and meters had to be invented too, but most of us never realized this.

Invent an industry, not just a product. VCs always look for a big upside to their investment and there's no bigger upside than inventing an entirely new industry. Edison is credited with creating a number of our largest modern industries. The argument can easily be made that he launched our modern electrical, music, and film industries. He also helped start the reprographic industry with his invention of the electric pen that could create documents from which multiple copies could be made. A.B. Dick of mimeograph fame acquired these patents and marketed his product as the Edison mimeograph.

I'd also like to suggest that Edison created another very lucrative modern industry: the industry of nostalgia. This industry thrives in a modern world that wants to remember the "good old days" of the pre-Edison world. Interior decorators love to display a wide variety of nonelectrical household objects to give a room that special, quaint feeling. Kerosene lamps, candles, and quilts all remind us of colder, darker times before the coming of electricity.

The industry of nostalgia was created by default when Edisonian products began to replace their technologically inferior predecessors. Kerosene lamps were thrown out by the case when the incandescent light bulb became the primary means for lighting homes and businesses. Water, wind, and steam-driven "mills" either closed down or adapted to the new electrical realities in order to compete. A surprising number of these old mills now serve as rural getaways for nostalgic couples. Chances are there's a mill-themed bed and breakfast—Summer's Mill, The Grist Mill, Fall's Mill-in most rural tourist destinations.

Finally, keep your competitors guessing. Edison may have been granted more patents than anyone else in American history, but that doesn't mean that he was an adoring fan of the patent system in the United States (or abroad). Edison was constantly dragged into court for patent lawsuits, usually by other people claiming that an Edison invention violated their existing patent. Although he understood the role of the patent system and usually triumphed in the battles, he grew weary and skeptical of the whole process.

As a result, he began thinking seriously about avoiding patents altogether and relying more on trade secrets as a source of competitive advantage. As he prepared to build his second lab in West Orange he declared, "I am so thoroughly convinced of the uselessness of patents that one of my objects in building my present laboratory is to search for trade secrets—particularly chemical processes—that require no patents, and may be sources of profit until some one else discovers them." Edison was wise enough as a businessman to realize that the complexity of a trade secret allowed you to bypass the public disclosure that accompanies a patent in exchange for a period of exclusive rights.

His viewpoint on this issue suggests that the most attractive investments are protected by trade secrets and other complex processes. In fact, some experts believe that trade secrets and other intangibles account for much of the difference between a company's market capitalization and its book value. Trade secrets like Colonel Harlan Sanders's secret recipe for Kentucky Fried Chicken or the formula for Coca-Cola have proven to be every bit as profitable as patented processes even though they are supposedly locked away in safes in their respective company headquarters.

NO MORE POKER FACES

A lot of businesspeople have played poker at some point in their life—most likely in college. If you've played poker, you're not alone in the business world since some very prominent American businessmen are known to have a great love for the game. Bill Gates was an adept poker player during his time at Harvard University and played regularly with his current Microsoft manager and then college roommate, Steve Ballmer. Likewise, Lee Iacocca wrote about his love of poker and his regular attendance at games in his best-selling autobiography.

The game of poker was invented in America so it's understandable that it's found a place in our business culture. More than one high-level business negotiation has been referred to as a "poker game" populated by "poker-faced" negotiators. Unfortunately, poker may be a poor metaphor for doing business and might hinder you in your ability to raise capital. You can enjoy poker on a regular basis and run a successful business. However, people who try to bring too many lessons from the poker table to the business table may find themselves at a disadvantage. Skeptical? Consider three ways that business and capital raising are different from a poker game:

Poker can never be a win-win proposition. We're all familiar with the terminology of win-win, win-lose, and lose-lose. Wars, especially civil wars, typically turn into lose-lose propositions. In contrast, it's common in business circles to focus on creating win-win propositions in which both parties can win as a result of engaging in mutually beneficial exchange. Poker is an entirely different story, however. It can never, ever be a win-win proposition because any money you win at the poker table is coming out of somebody else's pocket.

Think about it—at best, all the game of poker can do is redistribute existing wealth. It can never *create* new wealth, as people who are engaged in business do every day. Since it basically redistributes wealth, poker is similar to a tax system that takes money out of one person's pocket and puts it into

HONEST AL

Throughout American history, the truly great businesspeople have always agreed that one thing is central to success in business: honesty. Business greats from Benjamin Franklin forward have publicly acknowledged the importance of honesty in all business activities. Whereas some view business as nothing but a con game revolving around lies and dirty tricks, others view business as an arena where honesty and credibility pay significant long-term dividends. Edison was of the latter kind and he wanted to get the word out about how honesty in business pays great dividends.

In a 1923 interview in *Colliers* magazine, Edison left no doubt about his stance on this matter. He stated "Do you know that a completely honest man is getting to be a mighty hard person to find nowadays? I don't mean according to the standards of the law. A morally dishonest man may be a more dangerous citizen than a legally dishonest man. He doesn't have to be 100 percent crooked or 50 percent crooked to make him dangerous. A half-way honesty is a half-hearted honesty.

"[We need] to teach the business of honesty. We may try to disguise it as we will, but a large part of the world seems to believe that dishonesty is the only business policy with any money in it. This is the most dangerous theory in the youthful mind today, and there is only one way to explode it—by [teaching] the facts that have made our business and industrial leaders successful. We have to take our boys and girls behind the scenes of the world's work, and let them see for themselves the economic absurdity that any enduring success or happiness could be built on trickery or fraud or deceit."

someone else's pocket. Poker is a game of winners and losers whereas business can be a game of winners and winners.

Poker rewards the best liar. Contrary to what you might believe, poker is not a game of luck. Oh sure, there's what's known as "luck of the draw" as the cards are being dealt, but read any analysis of the game and you'll quickly discover that luck has very little to do with who wins money at the poker table. Most people think that since poker is gambling it involves luck and is like playing the roulette wheel or playing the lottery. Let's assume that poker is a game of luck (which it is not). If that were so, then the "luckiest person" at each table would win. Thus, the trick is to always be the luckiest person. This is clearly a ludicrous analysis since nobody is any more or less lucky than anybody else. Let's take a closer look at the dynamics of the game.

If everybody at the poker table is equally lucky, as I argue above, then the next best strategy at the poker table is to become a card counter. That is, you should bet when the probability of winning is highest and fold when the probability of winning is lowest. However, if everybody at the table can count cards with equal skill, what do you do to get an advantage?

The best strategy after card counting is called people reading. That is, the player who can best read the actions and reactions of the other players as the cards are dealt and bets are made will triumph. Thus, you'll find a lot of advanced poker players who are good students of what they call "human nature." They've learned how to watch reactions closely and predict how people are going to behave. But what if everybody at the table can both count cards and read people with equal skill?

The last and best strategy at this level of poker playing is lying. Poker advocates soften the language a bit by calling it "bluffing," but call it what you will, it's a deceptive strategy. At this level, you win in poker not for the cards you have in your hand but for the cards the other players *think* you have. Therefore, skilled poker players become skilled deceivers and can convince other players they're holding a royal flush when they really just have a pair of threes or vice versa. This is why you'll observe almost no emotion at the table when there's a game of professional poker players.

Poker rewards you for hiding your emotions. You don't need much supporting evidence on a statement like this when the most common idiom in the American language for an expressionless face is a "poker face." Nonetheless, I encourage you to watch a championship poker game on television sometime and observe how much emotion the top players in the world display while interacting with one another. You'll see a group of completely straight-faced individuals sitting around a table, slowly picking up the cards that are dealt to them and showing no emotion whatsoever until the game is over. This complete lack of expression and emotion is the logical end of the poker mentality.

I try to imagine what it would be like to do business with somebody who tried to maintain a poker mentality at the bargaining table. I might ask, "So, what are you interested in getting from this deal?" Their response: A blank stare. Then I might try, "Are you excited about our future possibilities?" Their response: A blank stare. So I try to stare back at them and they respond: "Now we're getting somewhere…." In contrast to the poker model of raising capital, Edison was constantly enthusiastic about his products and possibilities and this played no small part in his success in raising capital. He also offered a great upside for his investors and tended to keep a good line of communication flowing between him and them.

WAS EDISON A BAD BUSINESSMAN?

I've pointed out that Peter Drucker considered Edison the archetype of all high-tech entrepreneurs in America. I couldn't agree more. And Drucker and I are not the only ones to notice something special about Edison. Current e-business guru Jeff Bezos of Amazon.com was honored by being chosen as *Time* magazine's Person of the Year for 1999. When *Time* asked Bezos about his heroes, he named two: Walt Disney and Thomas Edison. I guess Drucker was right 15 years ago when he suggested that Edison would be a role model for high-tech entrepreneurs.

Both Drucker and Bezos qualified their admiration of Edison, however. In his interview with *Time*, Bezos observed that Edison was a "brilliant innovator and a horrid businessman." Drucker also admired Edison's inventiveness but argues that Edison failed miserably at being a business "tycoon." In the final analysis, I don't disagree with either one of these two great management gurus. Edison did indeed experience a great deal of difficulty trying to

THE BENEFIT OF NOT CAPTURING VALUE

One of the keys to creating a successful business is to both create and capture value. As noted, Edison was a master at creating value but less than perfect at capturing the value of his inventions. He didn't fail by any means as he lived comfortably and left a large estate. Nevertheless, his investors were the primary beneficiaries of his discoveries. This may not be all bad, however.

Today we underestimate the influence Edison wielded in his day. He was continually ranked among the most admired and valuable Americans in any public poll. The trouble with capturing every cent you can from your business is that your public image tends to suffer. For example, let's look at the defendants in two of America's best known anti-trust cases: Standard Oil and Microsoft. In many ways, it was not Standard Oil and Microsoft on trial as much as John D. Rockefeller and Bill Gates. In contrast to Edison, both Rockefeller and Gates were exceptionally good at both creating and capturing value. However, unlike Edison, both of their reputations took and continue to take a public beating.

make the leap from creator of innovative products and services to overseer of a sprawling industrial enterprise. You could also say he struggled mightily making the transition between Pre-Corporate America and Corporate America. He may indeed have been the archetypical high-tech entrepreneur, but he was not the archetypical "organizational man" that Alfred Sloan of General Motors turned out to be.

Edison was a *great* businessman by Pre-Corporate America's standards. However, he never completely mastered the rules for success in Corporate America. Thus, many people have concluded he wasn't a good businessman. This is a little like evaluating the athletic prowess of an Olympic archer according to the standards used to judge an Olympic pole vaulter, or vice versa. They're both great athletes according to the standards of their sports. However, each would fail miserably were they to be judged by the other's standard. The same goes for Edison. To judge him by how successful he was in capturing the value created by all of his inventions would be judging him in terms of Corporate America. Corporate America's John D. Rockefeller was a master at creating *and* capturing value. In contrast, Edison was a master at creating value.

It's been jokingly said that Edison made four fortunes: electric lighting, the phonograph, motion pictures, and J. P. Morgan's (the capitalist that financed the consolidation of Edison's electrical patents into what is now known as General Electric). In addition, Edison lost *all* of his electric lighting fortune on an ill-fated mining venture in which he wanted to revolutionize the mining of iron ore by using giant magnets to separate iron ore from rock. So from one perspective it looks like Edison was a poor businessman. Yet, it can be argued that Edison was willing to share the wealth he created and continued taking risks—big risks—even after his initial successes.

So just how wealthy was Edison? An August 1908 article in the *Albany Times-Union* reported his personal worth at $25 million and, if this is a correct estimate, it's an impressive achievement. We know for certain that at the time of his death in 1931, Edison's estate was worth $12 million. In contrast, the more organizationally-minded Rockefeller's wealth peaked at close to a billion dollars. Although that's quite a difference in wealth, Edison was most likely the wealthiest "inventor" of his day. Using inflation-adjusted dollars, his $12 million estate would be worth about $120 million today. That's good enough to place him within the wealthiest 1 percent of Americans in either his day or ours. Not bad for an "inventor." He was not a "master of industry" like Carnegie or John D. Rockefeller, but he was definitely the wealthiest high-tech entrepreneur of his day. Industrialists like Carnegie and Rockefeller made money so they could reinvest it in their businesses and make even more. Edison made money for one purpose—so he could keep inventing.

When people give Edison low marks in the business category, I suspect they're using the wrong yardstick. Let's compare him to the man with the greatest fortune to come out of Corporate America: John D. Rockefeller. You can't measure Edison's success in business the same way you measure Rockefeller's because Edison had very different goals than Rockefeller. Corporate America taught us all the important lesson of learning to capture the value you create. Rockefeller created enormous value in the American economy and deliberately designed systems to help him capture much of this value and put it in his own pocket.

Edison arguably created as much value as Rockefeller. Rockefeller dominated only one industry but Edison's name dominated three industries in his day. The difference between Edison and Rockefeller is that Edison never made it his goal to capture a large percentage of the value he created. He wasn't opposed to capturing value, he just never devoted much of his attention to it.

Both Edison and Rockefeller did business on their own terms but they were very, very different terms. And what were Edison's terms? First, Edison wanted to invent. Second, he wanted to use the money from his inventions to fund even more inventions. Finally, he wanted to maintain control of his inventive process. Edison historian Dr. Andre Millard referred to Edison's business as "the business of innovation." One of America's best-known historians, Stephen Ambrose, recommended in a recent interview in *Fast Company* magazine that corporate leaders should read a biography of Thomas

Edison for the simple reason that he "got things done"—as good of a definition of a businessperson as I've heard. (By the way, I recommend Paul Israel's
well-researched biography *Edison: A Life of Invention* (John Wiley & Sons,
1998).)

I still consider Edison the greatest manager ever in the business of innovation, but he leaves a lot to be desired as a role model for capturing the value
that he created. If nothing else, this book should convince you that Edison was
one of the most innovative minds of all time. And despite some rumors to the
contrary, he was also a good businessman. Nonetheless, his genius was clearly
one of invention and discovery rather than finance and administration. I'd
like to look at a few of the mistakes that Edison made in his business life in
hopes that Post-Corporate managers can learn from his failure just as he did.

MISTAKES WERE MADE

Yes, Thomas Edison made some mistakes—big mistakes—in his business life and the good news is that we can learn from them. One of his biggest
shortcomings was that he completely resisted second-generation improvements
on his inventions. He was the first mover with the phonograph, electrical system, and motion picture. However, the second generation of products from
his competitors were vastly superior to his originals. Rather than adapting to
the obvious new standard, Edison stubbornly clung to his first-generation
model and rode it to an early grave as a result. Here's how it happened with
each invention:

The phonograph. Edison's original phonograph was not the familiar disc phonograph with which we are all familiar. Rather, his original phonograph of
1877 and his "perfected" one of 1888 were both cylinder phonographs (see
picture on page 63—The Morning After?). That is, they both operated by
recording and playing back voice and music on a cylinder that looked much
like a tin can does today. Edison made a lot of money on his phonograph until

Emile Berliner introduced the disc phonograph during the 1890s. The disc phonograph would eventually win the day for two main reasons. First, unlike Edison's cylinders, Berliner's discs could be mass-manufactured using the same technology that mass-produced buttons for clothing. Second, customers immediately fell in love with the disc because it was much easier to store than the more bulky cylinders with their hollow core. This disc ultimately recorded music on both sides.

Electric lighting system. When Thomas Edison flipped the switch at his Pearl Street station in New York City in 1882, his was the only fully-operational electrical system on the planet. Soon after his accomplishment, competition set in. George Westinghouse began building electrical lighting systems that were superior to Edison's in one important way—Westinghouse used alternating current, whereas Edison used direct current.

So what's the big deal about having either direct or alternating current? Nothing, really, in the end. Both will light that bulb on your desk. However, there's a world of difference between direct and alternating current when it comes to generating and distributing massive amounts of electrical power. Edison built all of his systems around direct current. They were small, intimate affairs by today's standards. All electrical power was generated no more than about a mile from its final destination. Thus, Edison foresaw an electrical system with thousands of local generating stations delivering direct current to his customer's homes.

George Westinghouse had a different idea. Alternating current was unique in that it could be transmitted hundreds of miles between the place it was generated and where it was used. Thus, alternating current allowed for huge electric power generating plants to be built literally in the middle of nowhere and transmit almost unlimited amounts of power to end users. In other words, you could get economies of scale with alternating current that you couldn't get with direct current. It was the "mass-manufacturing" concept of the new electric power industry.

Both direct and alternating current could deliver power to end users, but alternating power could do it on a more competitive economic scale than Edison's beloved direct current. Alternating current went on to win the day and is still the type of current in use today.

Motion pictures. When Edison invented the motion picture in 1891, he launched what would become one of the most important industries of the 20th century. Yet, the motion picture industry began with a tall box-like machine rather curiously named the kinetoscope. For five cents, customers could peer into the kinetoscope and view a short film showing dancers or boxers or maybe animals. The machine was well-received and Edison started counting his nickels.

He strongly resisted, however, the new technology that came along took the image out of the wooden box the customer looked down into and projected it onto a screen that a hundred customers or more could watch at one time. He thought it a rather foolish idea but, for once, relented and licensed projector technology to replace his beloved kinetoscope. It was called the Edison Vitascope and the projected motion picture still remains the industry standard.

These three stories show that Edison never stopped to think if his technology was "technologically correct" several years after its invention. Being technologically correct means that you're constantly evaluating your current technology levels in light of new generations of product improvement that have hit the market since your first move. Edison knew how to win customers on the first move but ended up being his own worst enemy when it came to technological correctness. Here's the man responsible for the invention of the phonograph, electric lighting system, and motion picture and yet each of his inventions were technologically incorrect within just a few years of their popularization.

No discussion of Edison's shortcomings would be complete without including a section about his greatest blunder as a businessman. As we've already noted, he relied on a steady stream of capital to fund his creative activities. There was one project, however, that he bankrolled himself—and it's still known as Edison's Folly. This project was Edison's attempt to revolutionize the iron ore mining and milling industry by using huge magnets to separate iron from low-grade ore. Edison funded the entire venture with his own money and never, ever had to listen to anybody else's advice. The result? His revolution never occurred and he lost a fortune in the process.

Edison experienced trouble on this business venture for three reasons. First, he tried to play by the rules of Corporate America—and he couldn't do it. The mining venture was set up to exploit vast economies of scale much like Henry Ford's automobile plants. It was a huge, huge venture that ate money and would have paid off handsomely if it had succeeded. Second, Edison jumped into this venture without any counsel whatsoever. He funded it with his own capital and lost it all—about half of his existing fortune. It's ironic that as much as he and others hated working with capitalists, he crashed whenever he tried to fly without their counsel. Finally, Edison experienced trouble on this venture because he entered it without an exit in mind. The exit became apparent only when he ran so low on funds that it began to jeopardize his personal livelihood.

Edison's ill-fated mining venture suggests that any time he turned away from inventing and tried to incorporate the ideals of efficiency, standardization, and control, his enterprises took a turn for the worse. Yet, when others, like his good friend Henry Ford, made these concepts the foundation of their enterprises, they flourished (though Ford is not remembered for an organization that rapidly kicked out innovation after innovation). What's the difference? Edison was in the business of innovation and was very, very successful at it. However, whenever he attempted to enter the business of standardization his companies faltered. The businesses of innovation and standardization operate by very different sets of rules. I believe that Edison understood how both sets of rules worked, but failed to master the business of standardization as well as he mastered the business of innovation.

E IS FOR EDISON

Key Lesson: In a capitalist economy, whoever attracts the most capital wins.

- Do you treat your investors as an enemy rather than a partner? What contributions have they made to the company for which you could thank them?
- How can you lose your poker face and demonstrate passion and enthusiasm for your next funded project?
- What are you doing to manage your reputation so as to be a more attractive investment opportunity? What information can you send your current investors to help them feel more confident?
- Are your products and services technologically correct?

PART III

INTERVIEW WITH AN INNOVATOR

"The Age of Speed"

THE RATE OF CHANGE EDISON EXPERIENCED DURING HIS lifetime was far, far greater than what we have experienced in ours—regardless of how crazy we proclaim our times to be. In our lifetimes, we have seen the world move from a speed of minutes to seconds to nanoseconds. In contrast, Edison saw the world move from the speed of horseback to the speed of the airplane—a much greater leap. True to form, he quickly realized that people—or customers—would not be able to keep pace with this new rate of change. He therefore concluded that the world needed a new schoolmaster.

Surprising for his day, he concluded that the educator of the future was not the schoolteacher but the businessperson. That is, business could change the habits and aspirations of the average American citizen more effectively and more rapidly than the school system. In this interview Edison argues that the innovator's greatest challenge is to create in the public mind an image of a higher standard of living and a better life. He argues that people will be satisfied with the status quo and progress won't happen without innovative businesspeople.

A great underlying theme of this chapter is that technology gives us a larger life. Technology is often vilified as bringing misery into our lives. Edison believed that technology was one of the best things to happen to his world—particularly the invention and *popularization of the automobile by his friend Henry Ford. Edison also argues that people educate themselves when given the proper technology. I believe he was right. I find this to be one of Edison's most profound and far-reaching writings. This essay is required reading for anybody who wants to invent and market a new way of doing things.*

This is the age of speed—speed such as men had never dreamed before. We are annihilating distance—we are conquering not only the land and the sea but the air—we are doing in minutes what our grandfathers could not have done in days. They were not equipped mentally to grasp or to utilize the new order of things which burst upon them. Many of them did not seem to know at first what it was all about. If modern industry and invention expected to have a market for its products it had to turn school-master on an elaborate scale. It had to educate the world before it could sell the world. It had to show men how to think a little farther and a little faster before it could expect to interest them in how to buy.

It was necessary to create an understanding and appreciation of a higher standard of living—and then a desire for it—a demand to get more out of life on the part of several million individuals who would have been entirely satisfied with what they had. People used to be content with tin bath tubs and kerosene lamps. Most of the attendants at the Chicago World's Fair of 1892 had never used a telephone. Had you told farmers who voted for Bryan for president that in less than twenty years they would be driving to town in automobiles at forty or fifty miles an hour they would have thought you had been drinking too much hard cider.

But the main point is that society was satisfied with things as they were. There could be no progress until enough people could be made dissatisfied—and this could be done only when they were brought to think beyond the limits to which they were accustomed. The educator had to follow the inventor—the specialist in high pressure stimulation of the public imagination—and the salesman had to wait until his work was done.

We may term it commercialized education—but it has made its results felt. I should say that the thinking power of the average man has increased perhaps twenty-five per cent in the past ten to twenty years. And certainly it has always been low enough. It is astonishing what an effort it seems to be for many people to put their brains definitely and systematically to work. They seem to insist on somebody else—often anybody else—doing their thinking for them. That is why I regard the general mental stimulus we have seen in recent years as so significant. Several industrial factors have been definitely responsible—to mention only three of them, the motion pictures, the radio, and the automobile. Let us look at the automobile.

Most of us view the automobile principally as a great business and manufacturing achievement. It is—but it is a greater educational achievement. Next to the World War it has done more, perhaps, to jar people out of the ruts of commonplace thinking than almost any other factor in our history. This is not so much because of its stimulus to our transportation as because of its stimulus to our imagination. The great value of the automobile is not the fact that it has made it easier and quicker and cheaper to go to places but the fact that it has inspired several million people to go. It has caused them to move, to stir themselves, to get out and away, to wake up to what is going on about them. And any agency that would have moved some of them would be a public benefaction. Before the automobile it would have needed an earthquake. Many of them had never looked at a map since they left school.

We emphasize the slogan, "See America." But the automobile has done more than that. It has made a good many hundred thousand Americans see themselves and their neighbors—for the first time. It has set their gray matter to work. It has revealed to them how petty and meaningless their lives were becoming. In the beginning we were a pioneer people—a restless people. But when things came easier for us and we were able to make a comfortable living without much effort we began to lose our restlessness. The automobile is helping to restore it. And that is one of the most healthful signs of our generation.

Restlessness is discontent—and discontent is the first necessity of progress. Show me a thoroughly satisfied man—and I will show you a failure.

The important mission of the automobile is not the opening up of new geography—but the opening up of new opportunity. And if it has awakened enough people to the fact, all of the gasoline we have used has not been too much. The automobile has made better roads—but the best roads of progress it has made are not physical. They are those mystic paths which urge men into new worlds of imagination and incentive.

We have long since passed the age of the pedestrian. But the mental advance of society as a whole has not kept pace with our physical advance. We have come to take the wonders of invention as a matter of course—as we do everything else. But those who call this a sophisticated age are wrong. It is a perfunctory age. And it is so principally because the majority of people won't or can't think far enough to understand what it all means.

Physically, the world is moving faster than at any time since its creation and some of us may pause now and then to question our emphasis on physical speed, but if it serves to stir up our sluggish brain cells, if it makes it necessary for more of us to think in order to live, it is worth while.

The wheels of progress—especially those of the automobile—have worked results which might be called miracles. But their greatest service has been to raise the thinking capacity of society. If there is one evil in the world today for which there is no excuse it is the evil of stupidity. The most necessary task of civilization is to teach men how to think. It should be the primary purpose of our public schools. The world is moving too fast for them, they are cluttered up with too much red tape and precedent. We have too much red tape in all of our institutions. Our educational system—much of it—belongs in the time when we traveled by horse-back and canal boat.

Chapter 8

ALL PROMOTION IS
SELF-PROMOTION

E DISON WAS NOT THE FIRST PERSON TO INVENT THE LIGHT bulb. He was, however, the first to hold a press conference about the invention. To be considered successful, a new technology must be widely accepted by the public. Although technical merit is important, it's probably not the most important factor in the adoption of a new technology by the public at large. To gain public acceptance the incandescent bulb only had to displace kerosene—the most popular illuminant of its day. The technical battle was quick and decisive: incandescent bulbs simply burned brighter and cleaner than kerosene lamps. However, this often is not enough. When considering what to do with your new technology, learn a lesson from Edison and the rest of history: It's not the best technology that gets accepted but the best *promoted* technology.

It's difficult for modern readers to comprehend the awe in which his contemporaries held Edison as an inventor. His early innovations in the field of telegraphy, such as the stock ticker, were enough to make his name familiar among the Wall Street financiers and the scientific community. The *New York Sun* heralded Edison as "The Inventor of the Age" after his invention of the phonograph in 1877. By anyone's standard, the invention of the phonograph was enough to assure him a place in the Smithsonian and every American history textbook that would follow.

In 1878, when Edison followed the phonograph with the invention of an improved carbon transmitter that made Alexander Graham Bell's telephone marketable, he not only jump-started the telephone industry but also rose to a new status among inventors. His capacity for innovation would move him beyond the realm of genius and into that of the superhuman as people began to grope for words to explain his incredible creativity. Shortly after he invented the carbon telephone transmitter, the *New York Daily Graphic* ran an April Fool's Day news story headlined "Edison Invents a Machine That Will Feed the Human Race" and it was unquestionably repeated by other newspapers as serious news. Not long after this report, Edison ceased being an inventor and became a magician when the *New York Daily Graphic* proclaimed him to be "The Wizard of Menlo Park." He harnessed the aura of magic that surrounded his business ventures and used it to his advantage when it came to marketing his products. He even created a little "magic" from time to time.

IT MUST BE SOME KIND OF TRICK

Edison's first great innovation, the phonograph, certainly fit the "magical" description. It's not too much of an exaggeration to say that the phonograph was such an amazing invention that had Edison invented it 100 years earlier he probably would have been burned at the stake. Early reports of his amazing new "talking machine" were met with skepticism and people trekked to his Menlo Park lab by the trainload to observe this strange, new invention firsthand. A surprising number of people believed Edison's phonograph to be some sort of ventriloquist's trick. After all, Edison shared headlines with another famous American, P.T. Barnum.

One of the most notable nonbelievers was the Bishop John Vincent, founder of the prestigious Chautauqua Institution—a notable educational institute of both its day and ours. The bishop arrived at the lab and performed a thorough search of the building looking for hidden ventriloquists.

Not satisfied, he stepped up to the phonograph and spoke into it a rapid and complex string of obscure Hebrew names from the Old Testament. When the phonograph promptly played back the string of names, the bishop announced that it was indeed no fraud since nobody in the nation could have spoken those names back correctly. His official blessing was reported by *Scientific American.*

THE FIRST MAGIC KINGDOM

Anybody who has visited a Disney theme park has experienced the sense of magic that Disney is legendary for creating in his parks. When you walk through the main gates, you realize that you've just entered a very special place. Edison trumped Disney by more than half a century when he started promoting his incandescent bulb from his Menlo Park laboratory. Once he and his men had finally perfected the light bulb, they wired the entire Menlo Park laboratory, both indoors and outdoors.

When word got out in New York City that the "Wizard of Menlo Park" had done it again and invented the light bulb, they came in droves to see the seemingly miraculous invention. Crowds of people accustomed only to the dim orange glow of candles, kerosene, or natural gas stepped off the train at Menlo Park and into the first and only place on the entire planet where the clear white glow of incandescent bulbs illuminated the night. A light blanket of snow that night multiplied the effect and the Menlo Park lab sparkled. America and the world had seen nothing like it and as more news flowed out, more crowds flowed in. In fact, despite stormy weather, extra trains had to be ordered to handle the increase in traffic. The event was so successful that Edison had to start closing off buildings at the lab as excited crowds started trying to take home any memento they could find of the occasion.

Edison's flare for the dramatic and magical extended to his investors as well as his customers. During the long development process of the incandescent light bulb, some of his investors became nervous and he knew he

WHAT'S IN A NAME?

Probably the two most famous signatures in American history belong to John Hancock and Thomas Edison. Edison had a trademark signature that you're likely to recognize even today. Below are four different signatures for "Thomas A. Edison." See if you remember which one is Edison's trademark signature (answer located at the end of the sidebar):

1.

2.

3.

4.

Edison's name and signature were two of his most visible and valuable assets. Even today, his name suggests that something entrepreneurial and innovative exists in the firms that use it. For example, there's the New Jersey-based, technology-driven Edison Venture Capital Fund run by John Martinson. There's also the Edison Schools corporation which privately manages public schools. The name suggests that something nontraditional is happening within the classroom. By the way, if you guessed the third signature was Edison's, you remembered correctly.

needed to do something to keep the shareholders happy. Although he was yet to have a long-burning light bulb, he did have a number of working prototypes that could glow for several minutes before burning out and he decided to use these to renew his investor's confidence. The investors arrived at the Menlo Park lab at the end of the day and were greeted by Edison. He deliberately led them up a darkened stairway to the second floor of the lab. As the investors fumbled their way up the stairway in the dark, he clapped his hands twice and—presto!—the prototype bulbs surged with electricity and lit up the staircase.

An ordinary businessperson would have made the bulb prototypes the centerpiece of a long technical talk explaining the merits of the technology to the investors and pleading for more time. Not Edison. My favorite part of the story is his turning on the bulbs by clapping. Bringing the investors up a dark staircase was brilliant but clapping to give the signal to turn on the bulbs was simply over the top! Edison kept the promotional campaign going by lighting up the results of the 1880 presidential election with electric lights. Some even report that he arranged electrical parades through the streets of New York City to promote electricity as an exciting new technology.

Even though a century has passed since Edison was proclaimed "The Wizard of Menlo Park," people still like to believe in magic, especially when it comes to understanding complex processes. Science fiction writer Arthur C. Clarke, author of *2001: A Space Odyssey*, once wrote that "any sufficiently advanced technology is indistinguishable from magic."

EDISON AND THE EDITORS

Thomas Edison was media savvy; so much so that one biographer has called him "The Publicity Wizard of Menlo Park." He knew from personal experience what reporters liked to hear and how the news traveled around the country. As you may recall, Edison's first entrepreneurial activity as a boy was selling newspapers on the Grand Trunk railroad between Port Huron and

Detroit. Within a matter of months, he went from seller to publisher and began to write and print his own newspaper on board the train. A few years later he became a telegraph operator who sent vast amounts of news copy around the country in addition to a few personal messages. The telegraph industry was the center of the news world, much like television is today, and Edison understood what made interesting news.

From these experiences, he developed a keen marketing and promotion talent that aided him throughout his life. He often overextended himself to accommodate reporters who flocked to Menlo Park to see his latest inventions. Some of these reporters were personal friends from Edison's telegraph operator days and eager to help spread the word about their friend's new success. One in particular, Edwin Fox, shared an especially close relationship with Edison. Fox all but lived at the laboratories and constantly reported the breaking news about the latest inventions. Fox also served as a mentor and coach to Edison in helping him shape his media image.

Not all businessmen in Edison's day were treated as favorably. Men like financier Jay Gould and John D. Rockefeller were vilified in the press. Reporters were eager to find some dirt on businessmen, make some mud, and start slinging it around in order to increase the circulation of their newspapers. Although Edison had some minor downturns with the press, he is remembered more fondly because he understood the power of the media and made it work for him.

If you want to improve your media presence and reputation, Edison's life offers several valuable lessons. First, Edison forged friendly relationships with the vast majority of reporters that visited his lab. This sounds easy and obvious but most businesspeople fall short on a couple of counts. They either don't know any media workers at all or they manage the ones they do know with an arm's length relationship and phrases like "I have no comment on that," or "This is strictly off the record." Edison grew up in the media industry and understood that news reporting was a job just like any other. He didn't view reporters as inherently evil as some of us are prone to do. Rather, he saw news reporting as a job, just like invention. Reporters needed interesting, quotable copy and needed to report it as objectively as possible.

A second key for Edison was that he never mistook the press for a special division of his marketing department. I've spoken with newspaper editors who

LISTEN WITH YOUR TEETH
So Easy a Child Could Understand It

Spencer Tracy's film *Edison, the Man* begins with the kind, venerable Edison talking to a pair of young children who are interviewing him for a school newspaper. In addition to dispensing a good deal of sage advice, the elder Edison works to keep his language and explanations as simple as possible for the children's sake. Despite the historical inaccuracies of the rest of the film, the producers did a great job of portraying another key technique for improving creativity: talking with children.

The next time you need to kick-start your creativity, try explaining your current problem to a three- or four-year-old child. A couple of interesting things will happen. First, chances are you'll have to simplify the problem to its most basic parts. Second, you'll probably have to create an analogy to help the child grasp the problem in concepts he or she can understand (such as, "Well, Simone, think of it as trying to put a bulldozer inside of a giant bubble"). The act of simplifying a problem and creating analogies may yield significant new insight into the problem with which you are struggling.

There's also another important part of this process: Listen to whatever the child says back to you. A child can provide you with completely new and unbiased feedback on your problem. A big part of creativity is seeing the problem from a new perspective and listening to children can certainly help you do this.

share stories about local business leaders genuinely upset that the paper won't run a special story about the big sale that the company is going to be having next week. Through clenched teeth, the editors usually respond that they'd be happy to sell the company some advertising space but reserve their copy for news stories like grand openings, financial announcements, and downsizing announcements. Although he appreciated the power of the press, Edison never seemed to rely on it to carry his stories. Instead, he created fabulous inventions and staged trade show exhibits that gave the reporters the copy they needed for the next day's news.

A final media lesson from Edison's life comes from the nature of his relationship with reporter Edwin Fox. Edison formed a mentoring relationship with Fox in which Fox coached him toward greater media effectiveness. This

THE DEATH OF THE PERSONAL COMPUTER?

Pundits have been predicting the death of the personal computer (PC) for several years. With the increasing sophistication of the World Wide Web, visionaries like Oracle's Larry Ellison argue that PCs are now unnecessary. Why do you need a hard drive to store software applications that will be obsolete only months after you purchase them? Why not be networked into a mainframe system where a vast selection of software is continually available and updated? Why, the way we use and think about computers doesn't fit into that little PC box anymore, does it? Ellison has predicted that the home of the future will have a screen, keyboard, and mouse and a network connection to a vast mainframe computer located in, say, rural Nebraska, where all of the home's software and personal files are stored.

suggests that Edison didn't view himself as a natural media expert and that he had the humility to take some coaching from somebody who was involved in the business on a daily basis.

FEELING SAFE AND SECURE

One of the earliest promotional themes Edison used was safety. That is, he promoted electricity as a safer illumination source than candles, kerosene, natural gas, or arc-lighting. The argument against candles and kerosene was simple. These forms of lighting required an open flame for illumination. Electricity didn't, so it all but eliminated the threat of fire. Fire was a very real threat in those days. Almost everybody in the country knew that the better

Advocates of the PC aren't so quick to write off the traditional home-based hard drive. In fact, a little "safety first" thinking is all they need to swing the pendulum back toward a pro-PC mentality. Here's how it works: Would you feel comfortable knowing that all your financial documents are stored in a big computer in Nebraska that some hacker could break into? And those pictures of your children you've been storing on the mainframe, what if somebody got ahold of those and targeted your children? What if a tornado tears through Nebraska and you can't get access to all that software? The safest way is to keep everything locked up tight on your very own personal computer or server at your home, right?

Safety and security are key consumer motivators that can be used in a wide variety of promotional settings. Whatever your product or service, chances are you'll find a great promotional message if you put on your "safety hat" and do a little brainstorming.

part of Chicago had burned to the ground in 1871 as a result of a fire most likely started by a kerosene lantern used to light the O'Leary's barn.

Like candles and kerosene, natural gas also required an open flame but had an additional safety hazard. Should the flame get blown out, natural gas could continue to escape from the outlet and kill you—a danger well beyond candles and kerosene. Arc-lighting was safer and just as easy as other illumination methods, but requires a little more explanation. Arc-lighting worked similarly to the sparklers that we use to celebrate the Fourth of July holiday in America. It was a metal shell with a variety of carbon rods that glowed brilliantly when charged with electricity. The result was a brighter-than-day glow, but it also hissed, threw off embers, and couldn't be used indoors.

Like gas lighting, arc-lighting was contained within a secured fixture and couldn't be kicked over like a candle or a lantern. Arc-lighting improved upon gas lighting in that there was not any escaping gas to kill consumers when the flame went out. Unfortunately, arc-lighting could still kill you due to its open and uncontrolled electrical charge. Stories of unfortunate municipal repairmen getting roasted alive while working with or near arc-lighting systems were both frequent and widely circulated.

Given these competitive alternatives, Edison's safety message was simple: virtually no threat of fire, absolutely no escaping gas, and greater control of the electrical charge. His strongest promotional tactics focused on the message about better control. The telegraph industry had simply strung their wires in the open spaces between buildings, creating a safety hazard for anybody unfortunate enough to come into contact with one of them. Edison took great pains to bury his wires beneath the streets of Manhattan to promote his lighting system as a safer alternative. In addition, whereas arc-lighting relied on the equivalent of an electrical open-pit barbecue grill for its illumination, Edison was quick to point out that his lighting system was safely encased within the glass bulbs. The bulb might get hot, but you wouldn't get electrocuted if you bumped up against it like you would with an arc-lighting system.

WHAT WOULD OSCAR® SAY ABOUT THIS?

A final strategy you can use to promote your product is to promote excellence within the industry itself by giving awards for excellence. This might seem like a strange approach until you consider the best-known example of such a strategy: the Oscars. Since Edison basically invented the American film industry, it's only appropriate that this industry has mastered the art of self-promotion. Every March, the Academy of Motion Picture Arts and Sciences recognizes excellence in filmmaking by giving out the Academy Awards (otherwise known as the Oscars).   ▸

In March 2000, an estimated 79 million Americans tuned in to television to watch *American Beauty* walk away with five Oscars—pretty interesting considering that nowhere close to 79 million Americans had seen this film in theaters prior to the broadcast. The Academy Awards broadcast can demand a television audience rivaled only by major sporting events like the Super Bowl, World Cup, or Final Four in men's college basketball. The Academy Awards are currently broadcast in over 100 countries and the worldwide audience is believed to be in the hundreds of millions. Let's take a closer look at what's going on behind the scenes at the Academy Awards.

The Oscars were first presented in 1929 at a small banquet in a Los Angeles hotel. The 250 people in attendance had paid $10 for a ticket and all the winners were known in advance. Pretty humble beginnings for a media juggernaut that now revolves around the suspense of opening the envelope and announcing to whom the Oscar goes this year. Over the years, the Oscars gained more and more media attention and grew in size. In 1944 the awards were moved from a banquet to an auditorium to better accommodate the audience. In 1953, the awards were broadcast on television for the first time and there's been no looking back since. The media coverage begins in earnest in February, when Academy Award nominees are announced, and culminates on Oscar night which is a hybrid between a fashion show, talent show, and suspense movie.

VROOOM! VROOOOOOOOOOOOOOM!

Of the many notable people to be employed at an Edison-related company, Henry Ford is the most famous. Ford left home at age 16 and moved to Detroit where he held a variety of increasingly responsible engineering jobs. He ultimately became an engineer at the Edison Illuminating Company. He was fascinated with the "horseless carriages" that began to show up in America in the 1890s. While still employed by Edison, Ford spent his nights and weekends in the shed behind his home trying to build his own gas-powered automobile.

Late one night in 1896, Ford punched a large hole in the side of his shed and drove his first automobile out into the streets. He and Edison met shortly thereafter at a national meeting for Edison employees. Having heard of his engineer that had successfully built an automobile, Edison advised Ford to continue with his gas-

Just who is the Academy? The Academy of Motion Picture Arts and Sciences was established in 1927 and bills itself as a "professional honorary organization composed of over 6,000 motion picture craftsmen and women." Despite their relative invisibility to most Americans, Academy members are nothing other than film industry professionals whose most visible activity is to nominate and vote on the recipients of the Academy Awards. In the context of this chapter, the Academy should be viewed as a division of the film industry whose main role is to promote excellence in filmmaking by promoting the glamour, suspense, and excitement of winning an Oscar.

The idea of giving awards to the best film, technicians, and actors in the past year of filmmaking and then showcasing the glamour associated with it has worked brilliantly. The film industry is one of America's most competitive

powered designs and avoid trying to build an automobile powered by an electric battery. With the blessing of his new mentor, Ford attacked the problem with new gusto.

Promotion in the infant automobile industry took place at the racetrack—or at least in a large, flat field since racetracks didn't yet exist. Early innovators raced their machines and the victor's design was the one considered superior by the public. In fact, Henry Ford acquired the venture capital that started the Ford Motor Company after winning a well-attended race at Grosse Pointe, Michigan. The electric car could never compete with the speed and excitement of the gas-powered automobile. Even when Edison reversed his position years later and tried to market batteries large enough to power automobiles, it was too late. The gas-powered engine and the automobile race survived and evolved into our modern sport of auto racing.

industries worldwide and the promotional strategy associated with the Academy Awards has contributed to this dominance. Critics start the Oscar talk well over a year prior to the award ceremony by reviewing films and announcing a performance as "Oscar-worthy!" Throughout the year, tens of millions of Americans will flock to theaters to see movies and will come out making their Oscar predictions. When the nominees themselves are announced, the nominated films can expect a hefty increase in revenue. Best of all, the cycle repeats itself every year.

Other industries have imitated this idea but none have been as successful as the Oscars. The runner-up award goes to the Grammy awards in the music industry and the Emmy awards in the television industry. Other leisure-related industries like the book industry have self-promotional awards like the Pulitzer, National Book Award, and in children's literature the Newbury and Caldecott Medals. The automobile industry gives numerous awards for excellence in manufacturing and design, and the computer and software industries do the same.

THOMAS EDISON: CULTURAL ENGINEER

Science and invention fascinated Thomas Edison. He probably enjoyed these activities as much as some of us enjoy playing sports or pursuing a hobby. In the end, he found the business of innovation to be his main source of entertainment. However, he was not so naïve as to believe that others would share in this pleasure. In fact, he took deliberate steps to cultivate a playful and curious attitude about technological progress in the American culture at large.

Shortly after he invented the incandescent light bulb, Edison began thinking about not only how he could promote his new products, but also how he could promote the notion of scientific curiosity in general. He decided to create and edit a weekly magazine devoted to showcasing new technological discoveries. He had seen similar magazines concerned with literature and art attract huge followings and promote regular meetings among subscribers to discuss the ideas in the latest issue. Thus, in 1880 he launched *Science: A Weekly Journal of Scientific Progress.* He stayed involved with the magazine for almost two years and used it as a tool both to promote his own inventions and to foster a culture of scientific curiosity. Although he eventually broke with the magazine and went onto other things, it survives to this day as *Science,* a longtime player in the niche market for science magazines that includes *Scientific American, Popular Science,* and *Discover.*

Edison was wise enough to realize that scientific curiosity on a national scale probably won't just "happen." Rather, it must be created and fueled and magazines were a great way to do this. Several companies have attempted to do the same thing in modern times. Yahoo! launched *Yahoo! Internet Life* magazine to promote Internet culture with the hope that Yahoo!'s fortunes improve as the number and sophistication of Internet users increases. Starbucks launched a coffee-culture magazine called *Joe* that sold only in its stores, but stopped after just a few issues. Oprah Winfrey launched her own magazine, *O*, recently in an attempt to promote brand-Oprah beyond television and books.

At one point Edison proposed incorporating a firm known as the "Scientific Toy Company" for the express purpose of socializing children to find science and invention enjoyable. The products would have included such high-tech items as practice instruments for telegraph apprentices, electric locomotives, steam engines, and to awaken the tinkerer in girls throughout America, sewing machines. Edison later explained his thinking on this subject in a 1911 interview in *Century Magazine*. He noted that, "...there are great possibilities in starting the mind right with toys. Give [children] problems to work out that will make them think for themselves...a kind of scientific kindergarten." Although he never incorporated the "Scientific Toy Company," the idea indicates that he thought about the problem of promotion at the highest, most critical levels.

SHOW AND TELL

Trade shows are big events these days and some border on becoming household names. Two of the best known are COMDEX, the big event in the computer industry, and ShoWest, the main trade show for the motion picture industry. COMDEX bills itself as the most important educational event in the information technology industry and it's become the primary event in that industry where companies jockey with each other for product placement and promotion. COMDEX started as an annual event and has evolved into a trade show with dozens of events per year in many countries.

ShoWest is where all of the major studios start to roll out their annual offerings each year. Closed to the public, press reports from ShoWest about summer movies slowly leak out over the course of the conference and get passed on to the celebrity-loving public on the evening news and morning talk shows. Both ShoWest and COMDEX are known for spectacular and controversial events at booths as companies jockey for the attention of conference attendees and reporters. It might sound like a new phenomenon but it's not. Edison was involved in event-based promotions and created a number of them to promote his inventions.

One of his most successful events was the magical introduction of the light bulb at the Menlo Park lab mentioned earlier in this chapter. Edison realized that consumers can be heavily influenced by well-planned and dramatic promotional campaigns. His success shows that a new technology will be accepted more often on its presentation than on its technical merits. Edison also got a surprising amount of press out of the fabulous exhibits he designed at the trade shows of his day. In those days they were known not as trade shows but as exhibitions and expositions.

In both 1878 and 1889, Edison set up at the Paris Universal Exhibition to promote his new inventions. In 1878, his phonograph won him the Grand Prize and sales orders began pouring in as papers carried the story throughout the European continent. Again in 1889, Edison's phonograph was the centerpiece of a large exhibit showcasing all of his inventions. Each day some 30,000 people heard 25 phonographs speaking to them in dozens of languages—a true marvel of the age. Edison also whipped up incredible amounts of publicity with his fabulously lit booths at both the Paris International Electrical Exhibition in 1881 and the Philadelphia International Electrical Exhibition in 1884. The publicity he received at each of these trade shows only furthered his fame and sales figures.

NOW YOU SEE IT

People sometimes ask which of all of Edison's inventions I believe to be his most significant. Invariably they express surprise at my answer. I'm sure most expect me to answer with the light bulb since it is by far Edison's most heralded invention. Although the light bulb was a high-impact invention, it didn't radically change the world (although it did make it a lot less dark). Others might expect me to leverage my academic roots and choose some obscure invention—like his patented method of producing chlorinated rubber. But I don't do that, either. When asked what I believe to be Edison's most significant invention, my response is simple and certain: the motion picture.

AT SCHOOL WITH THOMAS EDISON

Edison understood the power of visual media and championed an idea he called "visual education." He also expressed some critical opinions of the shortcomings of most educational materials: "Most of our textbooks fail on two big counts. They are not sufficiently human, and their application is not sufficiently practical. Their tendency seems to be to look upon the whole process of education as a job of dull and uninteresting work—with the apparent argument that the duller and more uninteresting it is made the more credit there is for doing it."

Do these comments remind you of your high school or college education? It seems we've come to believe that the more dull the book and the fewer the pictures, the better the educational value. Edison never claimed that he wished to make education fun. To the contrary, he once said, "Education isn't play—and it can't be made to look like play. It is hard, hard work. But it can be made interesting work." To this day, reading for educational value remains hard work. However, I agree with Edison that it can be interesting work. He believed that education could be made as interesting and high impact as possible if it were as visual as possible.

Prior to the invention of the motion picture, almost all cultures were literary in nature. They depended upon the written word as essential to almost every part of the culture. The invention of the motion picture changed all that. We are now primarily a visual culture and there's no going back. To use a currently popular phrase, Edison's motion picture was a "disruptive technology." That is, it drastically altered the competitive landscape in one or more market segments.

Edison understood that visibility was key to getting the public to accept and buy any new technology. This goes well beyond promotional visibility—although that is clearly important—and into making an otherwise invisible technology visible to the average citizen. It could be argued that Edison should be remembered for popularizing electricity rather than inventing the light bulb. Yet the light bulb was his vehicle for making visible the otherwise invisible technology of electricity. Do you have electricity? Sure! Let me turn on my light bulb and show you.

A good example of this same kind of visibility are the recent advertisements from Nortel Networks. Nortel Networks makes computer and communication network infrastructure products that are usually hidden behind walls and in closets away from the public view. There's almost zero chance of brand recognition because only a handful of tech-support workers ever see the equipment. As a solution, Nortel Networks has begun an aggressive series of celebrity advertisements asking the question, "What do you want the Internet to be?" with everybody from major league baseball slugger Sammy Sosa ("Oportunidad. So no kid ever has to shine shoes like I did. Unless they actually want to.") to legendary rock musician Carlos Santana ("A road to a world with no borders, no boundaries, no flags, no countries. Where the heart is the only passport you carry.") providing an answer. Internet network specialist Cisco Systems also suffers from a severe degree of invisibility. Not to be left out, they launched an aggressive series of ads to build brand recognition centered around the theme "Empowering the Internet Generation."

ARE YOU INVISIBLE?

Invisibility can put you at a disadvantage in our visually-oriented world. Here's a good example. Let's say you are the maintenance manager for a multibuilding office complex. Your multibuilding office campus includes your own small power facility. The climate controls for all of the buildings are centralized at your department. If somebody is cold or hot, all they have to do is notify your department and you'll make all the necessary adjustments. Sounds easy, right? Not if you're invisible.

Here's what a typical call sounds like:

RRRRRRRRRING!

Hank: "Hello, Central Maintenance. This is Hank."

Judy: "Hi, this is Judy over in Marketing. It's terribly cold in our part of the building. Can you please turn up the temperature?"

Hank: "No problem, Judy. Hang on just a second." (SILENCE) "Ummm...Judy, our controls indicate that it's 72 degrees in your part of the building. So...ummmm...I don't know if I can take it any higher without causing some real discomfort over there."

Judy: "Well, I don't care what your controls say! I'm cold! What's it going to take to get you morons to understand that!?!?"

Hank: "Now hold on there Judy. There's no reason to get upset. Let me double-check things." (SILENCE) "Yep. That thermostat's working properly. It's definitely 72 degrees over in your part."

Judy: "Aaarrrgghh!" (Slams down the phone.)

Sound like a familiar conversation? Hank's got a great deal going for him. He's courteous, he doesn't jump to conclusions, and he's got some sophisticated technology that makes the job of controlling the climate at his office campus a relatively simple task. His biggest problem is that he's invisible.

Here's another way that conversation could have gone:

RRRRRRRRRING!

Hank: "Hello, Central Maintenance. This is Hank."
Judy: "Hi, this is Judy over in Marketing. It's terribly cold in our part of
the building. Can you please turn up the temperature?"
Hank: "No problem, Judy. I'll send somebody right over."
Judy: "Thanks."

Interestingly enough, Hank is just as concerned and responsive in check-ing his instruments as he is in sending somebody over to the building. How-ever, the simple act of sending someone to Judy's part of the building lets her know that he's responsive. The person sent might not do anything other than walk around with a clipboard and check all the thermostats, but Judy will feel like her needs are being met. When you're cold, the last thing you want to hear is somebody in another building telling you that you are not cold because their temperature gauge says so. When Hank sends somebody over, he stops being invisible and becomes visible.

Technology used to be huge. Remember Hoover Dam? It's a highly vis-ible technological accomplishment—albeit a bit remote. The same thing goes for the space program. Millions of Americans watched the launch of Apollo 11. But technology is becoming ever more invisible and "magical." The aver-age citizen has no idea how cell phones or zip disks work. For years, Intel's chips were encased deep inside computers until Andy Grove and his manage-ment team decided to become visible by putting those "Intel Inside" stickers on the computers that carried their chips. In doing so, they transformed what many considered a commodity into a branded product. So stop being so invisible and start getting visible.

E IS FOR EDISON

Key Lesson: The best-promoted technology will often beat the best
technology.

• What can you do with your product or service to give it an aura of magic?

- What are you doing to build relationships with the media? Is your current relationship friendly or hostile?
- Where have you become invisible or taken for granted despite your superior performance in this area? What are you doing to raise others' awareness of the necessity of your presence?

Chapter 9

LET FREEDOM RING (CHA-CHING!)

THOMAS EDISON HAD A HERO AND HIS NAME WAS THOMAS Paine. Thomas Paine may not be a household name anymore but he's still getting attention among the right people. In his book *Leading the Revolution,* strategy consultant Gary Hamel places Paine alongside more modern revolutionaries like Nelson Mandela, Václev Havel, Mahatma Gandhi, and Martin Luther King, Jr. as a role model for managers wishing to start an insurrection in their industries.

Paine is best known for publishing a little pamphlet called *Common Sense* in January 1776 and it is widely believed to be the spark that ignited the American Revolution. *Common Sense* was more than a pamphlet—it was a manifesto and it spread throughout the American Colonies like wildfire. In fact, it's often referred to as America's first best-seller. At a time when only three million people lived in the American Colonies, Paine sold at least 150,000 copies of *Common Sense* and maybe even half a million. The United States of America was a country born of revolution and Paine was the revolutionary's revolutionary.

Paine was brought to the American Colonies by none other than Benjamin Franklin. Franklin had a nose for talent and found Paine between jobs in London. Franklin convinced Paine to go to the American Colonies and wrote him a letter of reference. Paine arrived in Philadelphia in 1774 and with the help of Franklin's letter became executive editor of a new publication called the *Pennsylvania Magazine*. The *Pennsylvania Magazine* soon became the talk of the town, but Paine was only getting warmed up. He went on to harness the power of the media to promote his ideas and to take on an entrenched power. Sounds like Edison learned more than one lesson from Paine.

Paine's writings ended up on the Edison family bookshelf and the young Edison read them cover to cover. Paine struck a chord with Edison like few other writers. Maybe it was Paine's basic language and common sense reasoning that made him an "everyman's intellectual." Or perhaps it was that Paine was also an inventor. Most likely it was the fire with which Paine wrote about the idea of freedom that won Edison over. In a sense, freedom became the heart of many of Edison's endeavors. He once remarked, "My desire is to do everything within my power to further free the people from drudgery, and create the largest possible measure of happiness and prosperity." Spoken like a true revolutionary.

A SHORT HISTORY OF FREEDOM IN BUSINESS

Freedom. Revolutions have been fought in hopes of it. People have taken and continue to take dangerous voyages across oceans to get it. Some of our greatest books and speeches have been written in its honor. Mel Gibson has shed blood in many a film on its behalf. People pay money—big money—for freedom and not just buying their way past border guards. Consumers have given fortunes in exchange for it. And it may just be the single greatest thing your business could offer. Let me tell you some stories.

For centuries, people who lived in rural areas and worked on farms lived sunup to sundown. A few candles or maybe some whale oil in a lamp might serve to light the darkness but both of these options cast a pretty dim glow. In the late 1800s, John D. Rockefeller built the Standard Oil company and effectively tapped the rural kerosene market. For the first time in rural American history, the day did not end when the sun went down. Kerosene lamps allowed the rural population in America to extend their day beyond the daylight hours. Rockefeller gave them freedom from darkness and they gave him a fortune in return.

The railroads revolutionized transportation in America in the 1800s. Trains moved the American population around the continent more quickly than horse and wagon but there were some serious downsides. You could get places in record time, but only if that "place" had a railroad track running through it. Furthermore, you could never pick when you left on your trip.

THE FREEDOM TO REBEL

Edison is often referred to as the father of the electrical industry, music industry, and motion picture industry. But did you know that he could also lay rightful claim to being the father of the tattoo industry? In 1876, Edison patented a device he called the electric pen and marketed it to lawyers, insurance firms, and anybody else whose business consisted of duplicating numerous documents.

The sharp end of the electric pen poked small holes into a stencil sheet while the user wrote out their text on the page. This stencil could then be used as a template through which ink was pushed to make multiple copies of the same document. The electric pen and the accompanying duplication equipment was the forerunner of those old mimeograph machines (remember that smell?) and, subsequently, our modern day duplication industry.

In 1891, an inventor named Samuel O'Reilly took Edison's electric pen and patented a system that delivered ink directly to the end of the needle rather than having the ink applied later. Thus was born the tattoo pen and parents of teenagers all over America sighed a collective groan.

Your date and time of departure were chosen by the scheduler at the railroad. In the early 1900s, Henry Ford popularized the automobile. It coupled the freedom of the horse with the speed of the railroad. When the truck came along, businesses could locate themselves away from the railroad tracks for the first time in decades. Families could vacation wherever they wished and sleep as late as they wanted. Ford sold nothing other than freedom. Freedom to go where you wanted when you wanted, and his customers gave him a fortune in return.

There was a time in the dark ages of the 1970s when we were slaves to our television sets. We cared deeply about the people who lived on Walton Mountain and dutifully tuned in each week to see if this would be the episode when John Boy got to go off to college. We dared not be late for the programming or—worse yet—miss it altogether. If that were the case, we'd have to wait for reruns after the end of the season or—gasp!—rely on our friends to tell us what happened. Then along came a little invention called the videocassette recorder. Some of us bought Beta and some of us bought VHS but all of us bought our lives back. For the first time ever, we could record our favorite program and then watch it at our own convenience.

In the 1980s, people were trapped in their homes and offices when they wished to make a telephone call. Telephone wires from AT&T stretched all over the nation and carried all of the phone traffic and if you wanted to make a call, you had to be connected to one. That is until Bill McGowan and Craig McCaw kick-started the cellular phone industry. Suddenly, people were no longer connected to walls or desks when they made their calls. In fact, we were so unconnected that we started making calls in the strangest places—cars, restaurants, parks, and even movie theaters (much to the chagrin of the other people watching the movie).

There was a time in the 1990s when you could shop for weeks to find a book or compact disc. Of course you could always forego the shopping and *wait* for weeks while the clerk ordered (or more likely back-ordered) a copy for you, but that was even worse. More terrifying still, we had to buy our compact discs on faith, never having heard the music. And forget the critics, what did regular people think about this book I wanted to buy? Then along came Jeff Bezos and Amazon.com. For the first time ever, we could visit a store with over a million books and thousands of compact discs. And we could listen to the music and read the reviews by people just like us. We were free! Free to run up and down the virtual aisles as long as we pleased. And we could do it in our pajamas. At 3:30 A.M. With our cat. And those hyperlinks to other similar products…We suddenly had more choices than ever before and we were drunk with the possibilities.

The history of capitalism is a history of freedom. Business should be a liberating experience for all involved and our greatest businesspeople have understood this. Freedom has been at the heart of the American business experience starting with Benjamin Franklin and going through the present day. Here we bring some of these freedoms to light and remind you to build freedom into the heart of your business and products. Business may just be the greatest force for liberation that the world has ever known.

FREEDOM FROM CORPORATE AMERICA

The first kind of freedom that business brings us is freedom from the past. This is not to imply that the past is bad. To the contrary, most of us will still sit around and talk about the "good ol' days." The past is not bad, it's just the past. We can only talk about life in Corporate America because we no longer live in Corporate America. One strategy you can employ to more effectively compete in Post-Corporate America is to identify and jettison the cultural baggage from Corporate America when you try to reinvent the culture of your firm and its products and services. If I were to make a "most wanted" list from Corporate America, it would include:

The one best way. When Frederick W. Taylor, the father of scientific management, championed this idea in the early days of Corporate America, it was revolutionary. Companies the world over lacked a systematic approach to managing their production and people. Hiring employees was done randomly by finding "able-bodied men" on the street outside your factory. Taylor changed all this by experimenting with different ways of doing certain tasks and then choosing the "one best way" for everybody to adopt in the factory. Firms adopting Taylor's ideas experienced radical growth in both productivity and profits. The trouble with the "one best way" is that it worked best when there was "no one way" to do things. Once all firms began adopting the "one best way" practices of scientific management, the early adopters lost their competitive advantage. Post-Corporate America has the opportunity to transition from "one best way" to "many possible solutions." This was Edison's way before Corporate America arose and the blinders went on.

Mass manufacturing. I've already praised Henry Ford for freeing America from the tyranny of the train track and schedule. Nonetheless, we even need an antidote to Ford. Ford's ideas for mass manufacturing automobiles allowed more people than ever before to purchase them. He was considered quite a folk hero for having democratized an otherwise upper-class luxury.

Mass manufacturing still has some legs but there's a new model emerging and it goes by many names, but one is called lean manufacturing. Dell Computer has led the way by giving you just the computer you want when you want it. One size no longer fits all just as one way was never best.

Broadcasting. This term actually came from the agricultural economy before the advent of the mechanical tractor or planter. In its original sense, broadcasting happened when a farmer walked through his freshly-plowed field with his seed bag strapped over his shoulder and broadly cast handfuls of seed into the upturned soil. Needless to say there was a lot of waste involved in this process as the farmer later went through the field and chopped down the unnecessary plants with a hoe and tried to form something that resembled rows.

When the radio was invented and popularized in the early 1900s, the term broadcasting was used to represent the idea of building a big antenna over your radio station and letting your programming bleed out into the atmosphere with no real knowledge of where the "seed" would land and become fertile. Now we think in terms of channelcasting or narrowcasting instead of broadcasting. Channelcasters and narrowcasters specifically target a narrow market and provide a specialized service. The Web has allowed narrowcasters bigger markets than ever before and the diversity of offerings has exploded. Likewise, whereas television used to be three network channels, cable has made room for hundreds of narrower markets than broadcasting could accommodate.

Edison understood that personal technology was profitable technology. In one sense, his life could be interpreted as a series of ever more personal innovations that empowered consumers by giving them more freedom. For example, the light bulb banished darkness forever along with the constant threat of fire. Individuals could have just the light they wanted just when they wanted it.

FREEDOM OF CHOICE

Believe it or not, lotteries have not always been as popular as they are today. They arrived with the pilgrims and were very popular in Colonial America. Not only were they used to raise money for public projects, but prestigious universities like Harvard, Yale, and Princeton were funded, in part, by lottery money. Extreme corruption resulted in a complete prohibition of lotteries in the late 1800s. They were forgotten for a couple of generations and then resurfaced in 1964 when New Hampshire started a state lottery. The reintroduction of lotteries was not the grand success officials hoped it would be—that is, until New Jersey added the magic ingredient. Shortly after New Hampshire's reintroduction, New Jersey began running a lottery and let participants choose their numbers. Needless to say, it was a bigger success than New Hampshire's.

New Jersey succeeded where New Hampshire failed because they catered to what might be considered the greatest of all human needs—the need for control. As you know, a lottery drawing is a random event so there's nothing you can do to increase your chances of winning, right? The immutable Theory of Probabilities dictates that everybody has the same chance of winning. New Hampshire believed that since the winner was selected at random then your number should be too. However, New Jersey put the consumer in the driver's seat and that made all the difference. Even if winning the lottery is a completely random event, it doesn't have to feel like one. Getting to choose their own numbers let lottery ticket buyers feel as if they had some control over their random world—even if that was ultimately an illusion.

When cable television was revolutionized in the late '70s and '80s, pundits all over the nation predicted that in the future there could be up to 500 television channels. However, one futurist saw the situation more clearly than others and said, "In the future, there's going to be only one television channel. Just the one you want." By this he meant that the possibility existed that savvy marketers could bundle together your favorite shows and channels from the thousands of shows offered on hundreds of channels and deliver you just the channel that you want. You now see this same pattern of niche marketing with Web pages like My CNN or My Yahoo. The same principles of ownership and choice hold for the "My Computer" icon on your computer

Edison's phonograph exemplified the principle of the consumer having the music they wanted just when they wanted it. The consumer was no longer at the mercy of the civic orchestra, live performer, or radio announcer to determine their music. Edison understood that although the radio was a new technology and potentially more exciting than the phonograph, the phonograph would win in the end. He wrote, "I continually experiment with the phonograph, constantly improving it. There are those who fear that radio will kill it as a salable device, but I know better. People will continue to prefer what they hear without rather than with static and other interruptions and distractions. They will continue to desire to have carefully selected voices and well-chosen instrumentalists ready for their entertainment, rather than to trust to luck and the program-arranger at the broadcasting station."

People are more willing to settle for something other than their most desired outcome when they get to make the choice. This can also be good advice for getting innovative projects through bureaucratic objections. It's easy for somebody to reject a creative idea when it's framed as a traditional yes or no proposition or a threat. It's going to be harder for them to reject a well-framed proposal that offers them first choice. For example, which of the following proposals do you think would be more effective?

"If you don't listen to this new idea, I'll quit!"

"Should I try to sell this idea to an outside party or would you like to get first bite at it since you're my current employer?"

The latter is clearly the more attractive of the two proposals. Not only is it less threatening but it gives the listener a choice—and choice equals control and control equals commitment. Remember the basic rule: Give them two choices, both of which make you deliriously happy.

FREEDOM FROM MONOPOLY

John D. Rockefeller was one of the most feared businessmen of his day. It wasn't because he was an evil "robber baron." That was a label slapped on him by a historian a few years before he died. Rather, he was feared because he had built one of the most successful and effective companies in the brief history of American business: The Standard Oil Company of New Jersey. In fact, most history books still refer to Rockefeller as a monopolist. Although that point is still being debated, it is clear that he appeared invulnerable to almost everybody. I use the word "almost" because there was at least one person who believed that Rockefeller could be beat. That person was Thomas Edison.

There are two kinds of light in this world: natural and artificial. Natural light is produced by the sun but has one major drawback—when the sun goes down, all light-related activity must cease. Artificial light, in contrast, was invented to allow humankind to continue their activity after the sun went down each day. In the 1870s, the demand for artificial light was met primarily by candles, kerosene, and natural gas. Kerosene was the most popular of the three since it was easier than natural gas to distribute and provided more illumination than candles. It also dominated the rural markets where most of America lived. City dwellers might enjoy the benefits of natural gas but the pipes that distributed it stopped at the city limits.

Rockefeller's Standard Oil Company dominated the kerosene market in the latter half of the 19th century. However, Rockefeller's position as market leader became quite precarious when Edison invented the incandescent light bulb. When Edison began illuminating lower Manhattan, the good news about electric light spread rapidly. He organized a persuasive and intentional promotional campaign to woo customers away from kerosene and toward electricity. His sales force intentionally pointed out two key benefits of electricity over kerosene. First, electricity burned more brightly and cleanly than kerosene. Second, electricity significantly decreased the chance of home-destroying fires that came with using candles, kerosene, or natural gas for illumination. Using these strategies, Edison cracked the market of the most dominant firm of his time with a simple technological innovation.

As the popularity of the electric light bulb increased and electricity spread beyond urban areas, Rockefeller saw more and more threats to his market dominance. However, just as the illumination market was beginning to slip from his grasp, another market emerged rather unexpectedly. Mechanics in both Europe and America had begun to perfect a means of transportation known as "the horseless carriage." Rockefeller soon shifted his focus from the illumination market to the transportation market.

Much of the greatness and beauty of Edison's accomplishment lies in the simple fact that he beat Rockefeller by offering a more superior product and service. Edison didn't reach for any form of government regulation to solve his market penetration problem. The antitrust case that eventually broke

Rockefeller's Standard Oil empire in 1911 was initiated by journalists and politicians rather than competitors like Edison.

FREEDOM FROM WAR

As testament to his global fame, Edison received many of the highest honors awarded by a country. In addition to the Congressional Gold Medal in 1928 and the Medal of the Franklin Institute in 1915 in the United States, he also received high honors from Britain, Italy, Germany, and France—this last one being an induction into its legendary Legion of Honor. He also received academic acclaim from many American universities in the form of honorary doctorates, including degrees from such institutions as Rutgers, Princeton, Union College in Schenectady, New York, and Rollins College near his winter home in Fort Myers, Florida. I'd like to nominate Edison for one other award, albeit 70 years after his death: The Nobel Peace Prize. His inventions turned the telegraph from a weapon of war to a business necessity and that deserves some recognition.

Businesspeople have a fabulous history of taking military technologies and creating commercial uses for them. The telegraph and the Internet—two of the most revolutionary business technologies of all time—were initially developed for purposes of waging war. Business has a great track record in commercializing military technologies and using them to exchange goods and services rather than gunfire.

The telegraph was invented in France in the 1790s but didn't look much like the electrical telegraphs that Edison used. The first telegraphs were optical (rather than electrical) and consisted of large platforms with panels that could be used to send messages quickly across the countryside when accompanied by telescopes on the receiving end. Napolean Bonaparte viewed these early telegraphs as nothing short of revolutionary when it came to waging war since the next fastest way to send a message was by horse and messenger. An army in control of such a messaging system could speed reports about battle conditions around the country in a fraction of the time an enemy without a telegraph could.

The Internet was also developed with a military application in mind. A group of scientists funded by the U.S. government was charged to develop a communication infrastructure capable of surviving a nuclear strike. These scientists came up with the idea of a network of mainframe computers that could route messages along a complex web of connections. If one computer took a direct hit by a nuclear bomb, the messages could be rerouted through the web and ultimately arrive at their intended destination.

Both of these inventions were developed with limited military applications in mind. However, citizens and businesspeople who wanted to play with these new technologies popularized both. Telegraphs existed for 50 years before businessmen commercialized them as a way of quickly sending business and personal messages around the country. Likewise, the Internet existed for years before people wanting to trade music, personal messages, and products revolutionized it. It's amazing what peace can result from a commitment to freedom.

FREEDOM FROM CLUTTER

Clutter. Our lives are full of it. It invades our desks, our attics and closets, and our e-mail boxes and hard drives. Whether we admit it or not, many of us are slaves to clutter. We have to buy bigger homes and bigger hard drives to accommodate it. Some of us even go rent storage space or, its digital equivalent, computer storage space.

The desire for control and freedom from clutter can explain, in part, the Napster phenomenon. From one perspective, it could be argued that Napster users are hooligans who steal music by putting it out onto the World Wide Web and sharing it with anybody who wants to pick it up. This likens Napster users to shoplifters who take music from artists and record labels and give nothing in return. Yet there's another perspective on the issue: the one based on freedom.

EDISON'S FAMILY

Since I mentioned one of Edison's sons in this section, I thought you might want to know a bit about his family. Briefly, Edison married his first wife, Mary Stillwell, in 1871. He had employed her a few months earlier at one of his shorter-lived business ventures. Mary Stillwell bore Edison three children before she died in 1884: a daughter, Marion Estelle, in 1873; a son, Thomas Alva, Jr., in 1876; and another son, William Leslie, in 1878. Edison nicknamed his first two children "Dot" and "Dash" in honor of his days as a telegraph operator.

Edison married his second wife, Mina Miller, in 1886. Mina also bore Edison three children: a second daughter, Madeleine in 1888; a third son, Charles, in 1890; and a fourth son, Theodore Miller, in 1898. Edison's third son, Charles, probably garnered the most acclaim among the siblings as he went on to become president of his father's umbrella organization, Thomas A. Edison, Inc. Later, he was elected governor of New Jersey in 1940. Madeleine Edison bore her father four grandchildren before he passed away in 1931. The last of Edison's children, Theodore, passed away in 1992.

The freedom perspective argues that Napster users are tired of paying artificially high prices for compact discs containing one or two great songs and nine or ten mediocre ones (or worse). Napster liberates these people from the clutter that comes from filling your compact disc rack with music that you don't listen to 80 to 85 percent of the time. Napster allows a user to have just the music they want when they want it. Think about it. Which would you rather have 100 compact discs with 100 songs you listen to regularly and 900 songs you could care less about, or eight compact discs with the 100 songs you like the most and listen to all the time? No more scanning through dozens of discs and programming your favorite songs to play. Now it's just one great song after another.

Depending on your perspective, Napster is either a legal controversy or a liberating phenomenon. Hardcore Napster advocates blame the music industry for their own problems. Believe it or not, they would argue, there was a time in America—prior to the advent of the LP or long-playing record—that you bought only the songs you liked on small records called 45s (lingo for the 45 rotations per minute needed to play the music at the right tempo). These were the true golden years of music consumption before the coming of the Beatles and their successful concept albums that motivated studios to let *every* artist release a long-playing album.

The problem was that the idea driving most of the "concept" albums was "one catchy tune and nine bad ones, but we'll put a great picture on the front to make it better." Napster exists, the advocates say, to rid America once and for all of such musical clutter and return to just the music you want when you want it. If things keep going the way they are, artists may be able to bypass recording companies altogether and sell their music directly to users via the Web. Recently, the courts have not been kind to Napster, but Napster will be remembered as a revolutionary program that demanded action because it empowered consumers in new ways.

Edison understood the lack of freedom that can result from clutter and the liberation that comes from getting rid of it. On December 9, 1914, Edison and company experienced what many considered a terrible tragedy. In the middle of the push to bring an improved disc phonograph to market, a fire broke out at the West Orange complex and consumed not only the Phonograph Works building but damaged or destroyed 12 other buildings as well. The lab buildings, the inventive heart of the West Orange complex, were saved but Edison's most profitable manufacturing facility, the Phonograph Works, was completely destroyed.

Edison's response to the fire tells us a great deal about his character. He stood impassively at the perimeter of the flames with arms folded as fire companies from eight towns struggled with low water pressure in their efforts to put out the fire. In his biography on Edison, Matthew Josephson reported that when Edison's son, Charles, began to lament the loss of almost a million dollars of property and inventory, his father responded, "Oh shucks, it's all right. We've just got rid of a lot of old rubbish." The next day, Edison told one sympathizer, "I am 67; but not too old to make a fresh start. I've been through a lot of things like this. It prevents a man from being afflicted with *ennui.*"

That same day, Edison predicted with his usual vigor to the press that his company would be manufacturing phonographs again within ten days. Although the prediction proved a bit too optimistic, phonograph production began again by the end of January—a mere month and a half later. Edison took advantage of the complete destruction of his assembly line and redesigned it using production experts from his good friend Henry Ford's company.

Although I don't wish disaster on anybody, there's really nothing like it to lead you to a new level of freedom—that is, if you're willing. I've listened to several breast cancer survivors tell their stories and they all share a common thread. Like Edison, they all say that on the day they found out about their cancer, they quickly "got rid of a lot of old rubbish." One survivor had always wanted to own a horse and on that day she went out and bought one and let the winds of change blow the rubbish away.

FUTURE FREEDOMS

There was a time in America when we all had to use keyboards. People not only had to suffer through hours of typing classes but afterward remained mercilessly shackled to their computers throughout the workday. Then one day, voice-operated computers came along and set us free.

There was a time in America when we all bought our clothing off the rack in prespecified sizes. The waste was enormous. Every season, retailers

LISTEN WITH YOUR TEETH
Disagree With Traditional Wisdom

By now you've figured out that Edison was a pretty quotable fellow and that many of his quotes flew in the face of traditional wisdom. Maybe this is why the press loved to carry his interviews because he made such controversial copy. One habit you can develop to increase your own creativity is to disagree with traditional wisdom. *Fast Company* magazine has made it a habit in their regular column "The Consultant Debunking Unit" to question such well-worn gems as Wayne Gretzky's "Skate to where the puck is going, not to where it is," and "Bet on the jockey, not on the horse."

Let's try this one: Have you ever heard that "necessity is the mother of invention"? Thomas Edison's life teaches us otherwise. Edison was not motivated by need and desperation. He was motivated by the commercial rewards of inventing and the joy he experienced during the inventive process. In fact, he was known on occasion to dance when an inventive solution presented itself. He also built an organization that made invention fun and rewarding. Invention had a mother in Edison's life and her name was Nancy. She took good care of her boy, Alva, and saw that he never knew need. The confident young man that emerged from her home went on to invent the 20th century.

were forced to hold clearance sales to get rid of all of the overstocked and ill-fitting clothing that nobody wanted to buy. More than that, people had to loosen and tighten the clothing they purchased because it wasn't made to fit their body. Then one day, somebody created a business to manufacture just the clothes you need just when you need them. Now there is only one size and one style of clothing: just your size and just your style.

There was a time in America when we had to fly on airplanes to visit another state or country. People wasted days traveling to airports, waiting in airports, and getting out of airports. Not only that, you couldn't pick when you left but were subject to the scheduler at the airline company. Then one day, somebody came along and created the personal transporter business. Soon almost every home and business had one. All you had to do was step into the transporter and you could travel to just the place you wanted, just when you wanted to. Suddenly, more people than ever began to see the world and all the older people sat around and told stories about the time they had to fly across the Pacific Ocean. Like the train stations before them, all the airports were turned into restaurants and shopping boutiques.

There was a time in America when you spent hours mowing your lawn. Every weekend people all across America were forced to fire up old and noisy lawn mowers and walk across every inch of their lawn. Worse yet, some had to capture all the grass trimmings in bags and find a way to dispose of them. Then one day, somebody developed a grass and watering system that mowed the lawn for you. Everybody attached a tank to their outdoor watering systems and filled it with enzymes designed to eat certain types of blades of grass from top to bottom. You injected more or less enzymes into your system depending on how tall you wanted your lawn. Suddenly, more people than ever before began enjoying their lawns and all the older people sat around and told stories about how they used to have a tan line that started six inches above their ankles and ended six inches above their knees.

There was a time in America when you took the same medicine as everybody else. Pharmaceutical companies mass manufactured the same medicine for every patient, a sort of "one pill fits all." Then one day, we tapped our genetic code and for the first time people could have genetic profiles taken to catch identifiable diseases in the early stages. These profiles allowed pharmaceutical companies to customize medication just for you. It was delivered straight to your home the next day from the pharmaceutical lab.

There was a time in America when you couldn't be in two places at once. Well, you figure this one out....

E IS FOR EDISON

Key Lesson: The price of freedom is a premium most customers are willing to pay.

- How do your current products and services provide freedom to the consumer? What are you doing to let the consumer know about this?
- How are you using my company to fight for freedom? What threat to freedom have you helped eliminate in the past two years?
- What's the wildest form of freedom you can imagine in the future? What can your company do to make this a reality?

Chapter 10

STOP INNOVATING
AND START PLAYING

I N 1920, EDISON GAVE AN INTERVIEW IN HONOR OF HIS 73RD birthday and had this to say about his accomplishments:

Today, I am wondering what would have happened to me by now, if, 50 years ago, some fluent talker had converted me to the theory of the eight-hour day and convinced me that it was not fair to my fellow workers to put forth my best efforts in my work? I am glad that the eight-hour day had not been invented when I was a young man. If my life had been made up of eight-hour days, I don't believe I could have accomplished a great deal.

Corporate America was just getting its start when Edison made these comments, but he had already identified what he didn't like about it: an eight-hour a day, 9-to-5 mentality. Make no mistake: he loved his work and probably worked more than most of us might care to. The danger he saw in the eight-hour day was not so much that of less work but of work becoming just another routine.

Edison continued his interview by discussing his concern about such rule-driven routines. He stated:

This country would not amount to as much as it does, if the young men of 50 years ago had been afraid that they might earn more than they were paid. There were shirkers in those days, to be sure, but they didn't boast of it. The shirker tried to conceal or excuse his shiftlessness and lack of ambition. I am not against the eight-hour day, or any other thing that protects labor from exploitation at the hands of ruthless employers, but it makes me sad to see young Americans shackle their abilities by blindly conforming to rules which force the industrious man to keep in step with the shirker.

ROUTINE: THE CREATIVITY KILLER

Thomas Edison recognized routine as a creativity killer. When did he sleep? Whenever he got sleepy. When did he eat? Whenever he got hungry (often in the middle of the night). Since the coming of Corporate America, our world has become full of routine. This hasn't necessarily been all bad, but it has stamped out a lot of individuality and creativity. The big trouble with routine is that you stop asking questions and start taking orders—even written orders like "company policy."

Edison avoided the trappings of routine because he lived in a time when it did not exert the influence that it does today. The managers who established Corporate America ushered in a culture of routine that is still challenging to break free of. The mass merchandisers socialized us to pay the price posted on the tag because it was so cheap and a lack of bargaining allowed them to process more customers. The food industry socialized us to eat three meals a day with one serving of food from each of the four food groups. Our parents socialized us to sleep as much as possible so they could have a little time off (this is a dirty secret that I'm privileged to, now that I'm a parent). The good news is that you can break free of all this socialization.

Let's take just the basic exchanges. I like to challenge the students in my negotiations class early on with a question like, "Did you know that you've been socialized to be little other than a nonquestioning robot? Let's take something as simple as prices. Which of you purchased something for breakfast on the way to class this morning?" Some brave student will raise her hand. "What did you have?" I ask her. She reluctantly tells the rest of the class that she stopped at a convenience store for some orange juice and a honeybun. "Did you negotiate with the cashier about the price?" Of course not, she answers. "Well, why not?" Silence. "Because you're a nonquestioning robot, that's why...."

Now, it's not my goal to be an unnecessarily mean professor (and these questions are a long, long way from being mean). I do, however, wish to challenge my students' most basic assumptions about why they do what they do. The conversation above evolves into a discussion about why most Americans willingly and unquestioningly pay full retail price for most items they

THE HIGH COST OF KEEPING A ROUTINE

Corporate America has taught us to live and die by routine, but I encourage you to consider that scheduling your life might be overrated. Have you ever heard the quote "A lack of planning on your part does not constitute an emergency on my part"? Maybe you've even tacked it up in your office or on the outside of your cubicle or faxed it to a harried friend in another organization. Such a saying makes perfect sense in the middle of Organizational America. At the close of Chapter 6, I challenged you to make it a habit to disagree with traditional wisdom like this. Here's a little motivation for you.

Once upon a time, there was a businessman who questioned this traditional wisdom and created a great business out of it. That businessman was Frederick W. Smith and his business is now known as the FedEx Corporation. Smith didn't view the breakdown of scheduling in Corporate America as a problem to be better managed. Rather, he saw it as an opportunity to be exploited.

209

purchase when the majority of the world's population bargains and barters during almost every transaction. Although I don't negotiate for my breakfast every morning, I have learned to start asking more questions and order off the menu from time to time.

By and large, many Americans pay the price listed on the price tag because we've been socialized to do so over the last 100 years. Price tags are great for retailers because they short-circuit the bargaining process by signaling the retailer's "take-it-or-leave-it price." The good news is that this was a great stimulus for our economy in Corporate America as it significantly lowered transaction costs. The bad news is that price tags stiffened the purchasing process into a routine and stamped out much of the creative deal-making that is the heart of capitalism.

The students in my negotiating class quickly learn that even prices listed on tags are negotiable. Everything's negotiable if you're willing to do it courteously and with a smile on your face. They're shocked to discover that they've been paying full price for years when they didn't have to—all because they stopped questioning the routine. In negotiating and business, value creation starts when routine is recognized for what it is and creativity is allowed back into the picture.

Creativity begins with the 1,001 small decisions you make each and every day. Consider exhibiting a little creativity next time you order some food. When my son Ellis was three years old, he ordered a bean and cheese burrito at Taco Bell in a very unique way. He stepped up to the counter and said, "I want a bean and cheese burrito with no onions, tomatoes, or spinach!" Everyday creativity is so simple even a child can do it.

Each new day is a chance to foster creativity by breaking with your normal routines. I've been known to challenge students to sit in a different chair each day when they come to my class. I got the idea from one of my college professors who challenged me to choose a different place to start shaving on my face each day. It can be as simple as finding a new radio station or taking a new route to work. This also extends to other areas of your life and work. Why do we sleep eight hours per night? Why do we eat three meals a day? I had to ask myself this last question just a few years ago…and I learned a great deal from my answer.

HOW TO EAT YOUR WAY OUT OF YOUR ROUTINE

In the fall of 1998, I received some revolutionary advice that changed my eating habits dramatically. Furthermore I received this advice in the most unlikely place—a women's class at my church. Quite frankly, the last place I would expect to find such life-changing advice would be when I'm the only male crashing a class known as *The Weigh Down Workshop*. This probably deserves a brief explanation.

Most of my life, I've been known as a pretty thin fellow—and I still am. However, a few years ago I had managed to put on about ten pounds of extra weight. I came across Gwen Shamblin's *Weigh Down Workshop* and decided to attend the local group meeting at my church on Wednesday evenings. Little did I know that I was about to have a genuine learning experience. Gwen Shamblin is a registered dietitian who started a highly successful weight loss program. Her advice is deceptively simple and totally Edisonian: Eat when you're hungry and stop when you're full.

Pretty strange advice, huh? All of my life I had been eating breakfast at 7:00 A.M., lunch at noon, and dinner at 6:00 P.M. whether I was hungry or not. I ate because it was "time to eat" and not because I was hungry. Everybody knows you're supposed to eat three times a day, right? Well, I've since learned that a surprising percentage of the earth's population eats twice or even (gasp!) once a day—and (I swear I'm not making this up) some of them don't even drink milk! Not only that, but Gwen Shamblin seems intent on getting the word out in America that you may not need three meals per day. She thinks your body will tell you when you want to eat if you just learn to follow its promptings.

Shamblin challenges us to set aside the artificial schedules that control our eating and reclaim our own natural schedules. Much to my surprise, I found her advice to be right on target. Eating's not the only place we've substituted artificial rhythms for natural ones. The modern workplace has been drawn and quartered for so long that most people think a 40-hour work week is a physical rather than a federal law. Edison never worked what we would call a "40-hour week" for the simple reason that the "40-hour week" didn't exist in Pre-Corporate America. He might have worked only 40 hours some weeks, but these hours may have been at night or all in one stretch.

A BRIEF HISTORY OF TIME

Why do we work during the week and take the weekends off? Where did the 9-to-5 schedule come from and why do we still think in terms of a 40-hour work week? Why do we dismiss school in the summertime? For that matter, why do I think I have to sleep at night and work during the day? These are good questions—even the last one—and they deserve good answers. Put simply, Corporate America saddled us with a uniform set of work rhythms that only a handful of people stop to question. These rhythms all arose after Edison's day. Here are a few of the most influential:

Agricultural history. The Agricultural Revolution was one of the first great cultural shifts in human history. When humans began to cultivate and harvest their own food, time began to take its current form. The dominant American industry used to be agriculture. In fact, Thomas Jefferson envisioned America as a nation of farmers serving as the world's breadbasket. Thankfully, people like Alexander Hamilton disagreed with Jefferson's view and believed that America could also industrialize if we put our minds to it.

Since the Agricultural Revolution, we've gone through the Industrial Revolution and the Digital Revolution. Nonetheless, the Agricultural Revolution is still with us. Public schools used to dismiss in the summertime so children could go home and help with planting and harvesting. Now our schools dismiss in the summer so children can return home because…because…well, they've just always been out in the summer.

We work during the day because that's when the sun is up. However, since Edison invented the light bulb it no longer matters if the sun is up or not when we're working indoors. Yet we all still work during the day without questioning this. H.G. Wells, an early science-fiction pioneer, wrote a short story called "The Country of the Blind" describing a land where everybody was blind and the culture that would arise under such constraints. One of the most peculiar things is that everybody in this country worked in the fields planting and harvesting food at night. Why? Because it was cooler at night and they didn't need the sun to see because they were blind. Thus the culture worked during the night and slept during the heat of the day.

Federal laws. From the early 1900s to the present day, a deluge of federal laws have shaped the rhythms of our workplace in rather uniform ways. One of the most influential and long-lasting has been the Fair Labor Standards Act (FLSA) of 1938. Despite talk of reform, this law continues to stifle a remarkable amount of creativity and individuality in the Post-Corporate American workplace. The FLSA regulates our work week and established 40 hours as standard in 1938. Anything beyond 40 hours would result in overtime pay. Worse yet, these 40 hours have to be completed in five eight-hour segments rather than the ten four-hour segments that might be better for a single mother or the two 20-hour segments that might better serve the interests of a programmer.

Tragically, most people live for five o'clock and the weekends when they don't have to work. I don't say this from the perspective of a workaholic but from the perspective of capturing the benefits of inspiration. When Edison and his team of workers were in the middle of an experiment, the last thing they would do is drop it because it was five o'clock. You don't manage inspiration, you manage around inspiration. Edison was known to work for days on end when the inventive fever had grasped the lab. If he needed sleep he grabbed a quick nap on a table or in a chair.

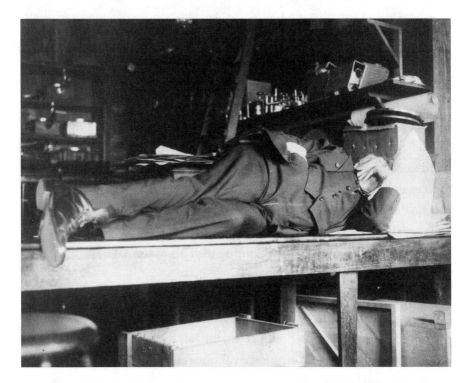

A PHOTO OF EDISON ASLEEP UPON ONE OF THE WORKBENCHES IN HIS LAB.
(Photo courtesy of U.S. Department of the Interior, National Park Service,
Edison National Historic Site)

The culture of efficiency. The culture of Corporate America promoted standardization and efficiency. One way it tried to do this was to get everybody to show up for work at the same time because…because…well, if everybody was there at the same time it just seemed more efficient. As a result, the flexible work schedules that Edison and his colleagues enjoyed were replaced by ones that dictated that all important work be done between the hours of 9:00 A.M. and 5:00 P.M. with a one-hour break for lunch between noon and 1:00 P.M. What if inspiration strikes at 11:00 P.M.? Too bad, buddy. You're supposed to be asleep by then. Routine will kill your creativity. It is efficient and successfully isolates you from any new influence.

THOSE CRAZY KIDS

Some things never change: death, taxes, and those crazy kids. Each generation of Americans has voiced their beliefs that "those crazy kids" are going to be the death of this great nation. Americans believed it in the roaring '20s when "those crazy kids" were all flappers and again in the 1950s when "those crazy kids" were all starting to look like juvenile delinquents in the movies. Of course, in the '70s, "those crazy kids" were the worst yet with their long hair and short skirts. And in the '90s, "those crazy kids" all wore short hair, tattoos, and multiple body piercings.

Thomas Edison was optimistic about "those crazy kids" and everything that they embodied. In a 1926 interview in *The Forum* magazine titled "Youth of Today and Tomorrow," Edison aired a number of views about the state of young America and concerns about the "dancing craze" and the mysterious "prevailing unrest." Concerning the dancing craze Edison said, "Most of us are so prone, as we grow older, to criticize youth for everything it does, forgetting how much worse we did when we were young. A wave of such complaint sweeps over Europe and America today, and most of it is foolish. For instance, there are those who predict the direst consequences from the increased vogue of dancing. People have danced ever since the most remote days recorded in history and if it has wrecked the race, as each generation of old fogies in turn has predicted that it would, the wrecked race, everything considered, is getting along nicely. The dancing craze, as it is called, will keep on, for it is perfectly natural. It really is by no means a 'craze.'"

Having dispatched the worries about the dangers of dancing, Edison went on to address the "prevailing unrest." He noted, "One of the many other things about that which we call current thought is that people speak of a prevailing unrest, applying this term particularly to the mental state of young people. It is not unrest in the bad sense in which the word is used that keeps young people moving, thinking, doing. It is, however, the opposite of stagnation and that is a fine thing for the world. The steady increase of activity is mostly orderly, aspiring, and worthwhile, having been brought about by those changes in the methods of our lives which can be attributed to new inventions and methods."

Edison remained an advocate of youth until his death and there are several things worth noting about his above comments. First, with regards to dancing, he reminded us that dire predictions have accompanied spontaneous activity like dancing for centuries and the human race has somehow managed to survive and even flourish despite the constant threat of beginning to shimmy when the music starts (although Edison might have changed his mind on this point had he lived to experience disco). Second, he takes the notion of the prevailing unrest and makes it positive in contrast to the habit of stagnation enjoyed by older, more critical people of his day. Finally, he exuded an extreme optimism throughout the interview about the youth of America. The 79-year-old Edison blessed the energy, spontaneity, and new ideas that pour from the young and generally believed them to be the most intelligent generation our country has ever produced. He gave this blessing because energy, spontaneity, and new ideas still poured from him.

This complete optimism about the youth of America showed in his concluding comments of the interview. He said, "The fact that the young people of today, generally speaking, are more intelligent than the young people of 1890, for example, when I, myself, was 43-years-old, is a pretty good guarantee that the young people of 36 years in the future will be more intelligent than those of today. What young people may be a century from now I do not care to predict, nor do I dare. They will be an improvement on the young people of the present. That is all I feel it safe to say. I am very hopeful of the next generation in America and of the many generations which will follow it."

ARE YOU HAVING FUN YET?

Would you like to know a quick test to determine how well your firm is handling the transition from Corporate America to Post-Corporate America?

Here it is: How well does your company tolerate young people? When I was in kindergarten we had a category on our report cards known as "Plays Well With Children." If this same category had been on company report cards in Corporate America, most of the companies would have scored a big, fat "F."

A surprising number of the most important businesses in American history were either founded or profoundly influenced by people under 30 years of age: Dell Computer, Ford Motor Company, and The Walt Disney Company. Youth has its advantages and these advantages have been economical ones in the marketplace of Post-Corporate America. This chapter is about recapturing the advantages of youth. Specifically, it's about rediscovering a sense of play, getting rid of our schedules, and restoring some spontaneity.

Consider the brief history of the Internet. Do you remember the first time you saw a Web page? I do, and it was a picture of rock-and-roll star Eddie Van Halen. It was in the fall of 1994 and I was in a computer lab at Texas A&M University waiting in line for a big, thick, professional statistics printout. I glanced to my left and noticed a computer with a full-color image of Eddie Van Halen brandishing his trademark red guitar. I had never seen anything like this on a computer and quickly learned that the picture had been pulled off a "fan page" somewhere on the "World Wide Web" using a program called "Mosaic." Mosaic went on to become Netscape and the World Wide Web transformed business as we know it. Oh yeah, and Eddie Van Halen became part of this book.

What does Eddie Van Halen have to do with Thomas Edison? For starters, both of their lives have revolved around electricity—one with electric light bulbs and the other with electric guitars. More significantly, Eddie Van Halen's picture on the World Wide Web represents one of the most important uses of a new technology like the Internet: play. As critical as the Internet has become to our current business infrastructure, it got it's start with people just playing around doing things like building graphic-laden fan pages for Eddie Van Halen and swapping Grateful Dead tunes.

Play might well be one of the most important activities you can under-take in Post-Corporate America. I don't want to overstate the point but the better part of Silicon Valley was created by kids playing around in their garages and dorm rooms rather than serious adults conducting serious meet-ings in serious office buildings. Corporate America preached the gospel of serious, rational strategic planning—and serious, rational strategic planning can certainly help your company succeed. However, playing around may be another legitimate route to innovative business ideas.

Did you know that at least one multibillion dollar business grew out of the unique hobby of collecting Pez Candy dispensers? Pez is a tangy, pellet-shaped candy produced in four flavors: orange, grape, lemon, and strawberry. When it comes to Pez, however, it's not the candy that matters but the dis-penser. For decades, Pez candy has been dispensed in unique, collectible con-tainers featuring character heads like Uncle Sam, Darth Vader, Bugs Bunny, Yosemite Sam, and even the Creature from the Black Lagoon. An interactive candy experience as wonderful as this is sure to spawn collectors and Pez has more than its fair share of them; they're known as Pezheads.

Pierre Omidyar's fiancée, Pam, was a Pezhead and being a good fiancé he wanted to feed that Pez passion as much as he could. Little did he know that he would create one of the great business innovations of the Internet economy. Omidyar and his fiancée were early Internet enthusiasts and she commented to him that it would be great if she could meet other Pezheads on the Internet and buy and sell hard-to-find Pez dispensers. Keep in mind that we're not talking oil, steel, or pork belly futures here—we're talking plastic candy dis-pensers with character heads. In the end Omidyar created a page called Web Auction where buyers and sellers of Pez dispensers and other items could exchange goods with one another. Traffic became so heavy that Omidyar started charging transaction fees and made the site his full-time job. He changed the name to eBay (short for Electronic Bay as in the San Francisco Bay Area) in September 1995. Pezheads worldwide haven't been the same since—and nei-ther have the rest of us.

πr^2 OR PIE ARE ROUND?

Why are some businesses more creative than others? Edison once explained to newspaper reporters why a certain group of individuals, in his opinion, seemed less creative than another. His answer was the quotable Edison at his best: "They don't eat enough pie. To invent, your system must be all out of order, and there is nothing that will do that like good old-fashioned American pie."

Research scientists are still determining whether or not "good old-fashioned American pie" can actually make you more creative. (Personally, I conduct an experiment on this matter as often as I can after dinner.) Until that time, we'll have to rely on Edison's core idea about getting your system "all out of order." His comment to the reporters could also be read as a clever commentary against the standardization, efficiency, and control of Corporate America. For the true Corporate American, nothing is ever "out of order."

Edison's life teaches us that creativity is a lifestyle commitment. It's using the 1,001 decisions you make every day to turn your life in a new direction. So what can you do to get your system out of order? Here are a few ideas:

- Live in California for a while because there's everything: every nationality, sun, water, forest, snow, desert, and the highest and lowest places in the lower 48 United States.
- Take a new route to work some day. Don't just drive a new way but travel via a different form of transportation, if possible.
- Listen to music that you might not otherwise hear. Try to make your own collection be at least one-quarter music with lyrics not in your native tongue. Check out recording labels that specialize in international music like Real World Records or Six Degrees Records. Also, try listening to some of America's great genre-busting bands like Brave Combo or Los Lobos.
- Go watch an international film. You know, something with subtitles. The surprise hit movie *Crouching Tiger, Hidden Dragon* was a great

introduction to Chinese culture for many people but you can go further. Try watching some of the films of the great Chinese director Zhang Yimou, especially *To Live* and *Raise the Red Lantern*. Edison invented the motion picture partly to help people cross boundaries without traveling as much.

• Instead of reading adult books, try reading some children's books to see the world from a different point of view. Check out the recent Caldecott Medal winners *Joseph Had a Little Overcoat* by Simms Taback and *Officer Buckle and Gloria* by Peggy Rathmann, or the wildly creative *Weslandia* by Paul Fleischman and Kevin Hawkes.

• Eat food that you're not accustomed to. Try having International Food Awareness Month where you go out for dinner at a different ethnic restaurant each week. In one month you can sample four new cultures and you should try for one on every continent.

• Read a magazine that you might not otherwise read. If you're into bird watching then try a magazine on auto racing. If you're into auto racing then try a magazine on quilting. If you're into quilting then read a magazine about business. By doing this, you might investigate some of the same problems from a different perspective.

"HEY, KALEIDOSCOPE BRAIN!"

What exactly did Edison do to reach the top of the invention heap and hold the world record for the number of patents? Although he had 1,093 patents to his name, they were not all in the same area. Had he limited himself to any one area—telegraphy, electricity, film technology—he would have cut his output by 60 percent or more. Edison never specialized in the sense that we know it today. He was a generalist and therefore crossed many boundaries.

One of his most remarkable creative aspects was the ability to conceive endless design variations for a particular product. One contemporary likened Edison's brain to a kaleidoscope—the popular children's toy that produces an endless array of colored patterns as you turn the barrel. The Western Union attorney, Edward Dickerson, described it this way: "He turns that head of his and these things come out as in a kaleidoscope, in various combinations, most of which are patentable."

Like a kaleidoscope, Edison began by putting an array of products in his head and then mixing them together into various combinations. One combination led to another combination. The more individual parts you add to the mix, the greater the number of possible combinations. Edison often involved himself in as many projects as possible as he found that one project fed into and improved upon another. When a problem stumped him, Edison would, "…just put it aside and go at something else; the first thing I know the very idea I wanted will come to me. Then I drop the other and go back to it and work it out."

What's one thing you could do to add to your creativity today? Try broadening your range of projects. When you get stuck on one, put it aside and do another and see if the solution emerges as the two projects cross-pollinate one another. You may end up with so many ideas you have to leave a few on the drawing board. In late 1889, Edison reprioritized his lab and left a number of interesting projects forever unfunded on the drawing board. That list included a cotton picker, a hearing aid, synthetic rubber, synthetic ivory, synthetic mother-of-pearl, synthetic silk, an improved typewriter, and a flying machine. Bear in mind that he left his flying machine on the drawing boards a full decade before Orville and Wilber Wright made the first successful flight in 1903. Who knows how history might be different if Edison had chosen to pursue flying machines instead of motion pictures at this juncture.

HOW GAMES HAVE FUELED THE DIGITAL AGE

In a 1921 interview with *American Magazine,* Edison answered a reporter with:

Which do I consider my greatest invention? Well, my reply to that would be that I like the phonograph best. Doubtless this is because I love music. And then it has brought so much joy into millions of homes all over this country, and, indeed, all over the world. Music is so helpful to the human mind that it is naturally a source of satisfaction to me that I have helped in some way to make the very finest music available to millions who could not afford to pay the price and take the time neces-sary to hear the greatest artists sing and play.

Many inventions are not suitable for the people at large because of their carelessness. Before a thing can be marketed to the masses, it must be made practically foolproof. Its operation must be made extremely simple. That is one reason, I think, why the phonograph has been so universally adopted. Even a child can operate it. Another rea-son is that people are far more willing to pay for being amused than for anything else.

Edison is reminding us that customers like to have fun, too, and it might motivate much of their spending. He realized that people are more apt to embrace a new technology if it is fun to play with. This tactic is still in use today so let me give you a few examples from the computer industry. Every version of Windows that I can remember has included a set of games in the basic software package. You know…the infamous Freecell, Hearts, Mine-sweeper, and Solitaire package. It might be a conspiracy on Microsoft's part to undermine individual productivity in corporations all over the globe—but that's highly doubtful. More likely, it's a simple way to get people to embrace new technology. A surprising number of Americans were first introduced to the wonders of a Windows-driven PC with a mouse by playing a friendly game of solitaire.

It's quite possible that interests in games and gaming has propelled the computer and software industry to more innovation than it would have had should the computer be considered only a scientific tool. Our personal com-puters are better and faster than we ever could have imagined but probably not because of the demands of the business consumer. Rather, they are faster due to the demands of the pleasure consumer. Graphic-heavy, Web-based video games like Doom have resulted in personal computers that can manipulate a staggering amount of graphic information on a video screen while simultaneously processing a steady stream of commands to control movement within and between networked computers.

Simulation games like SimCity and The Sims have also contributed to increasing levels of technological sophistication. Probably the biggest developments in web and network-based innovation have come as a result of people wanting to share and trade music files on the Internet. Back in the mid-'80s, The WELL (acronym for the Whole Earth 'Lectric Link) was one of the earliest meeting places on the Internet and swapping Grateful Dead tunes and tapes was one of its primary activities. Since then, digital music files have increased in sophistication and bandwidth requirements have increased by necessity. The computer and video game industry has become one of America's largest and most profitable industries. Pretty impressive for an industry completely dedicated to play, huh?

Edison was masterful in his ability to get people to integrate innovative technologies into their personal lifestyles on a regular basis. His success was not accidental but rather the result of an intentional strategy: make it as amusing as possible. How do you get people to change their behavior? This is a good question that can take a variety of forms. How about, "How do you get customers to buy a new kind of product?" Or, "How do you get employees to try new ways of doing things?" Or maybe it's as close to home as, "How can I get myself to embrace change?" But this question may best be framed as "How can we make this more fun for the customer?"

Play is clearly an essential part of any innovative business culture. Play should also be an essential part of your customer's experience with your product or service. Play might actually be the next, big gateway to a greater number of customers. For example, a lot of people are wondering how and when the information and entertainment industries are going to converge. That is, when will we replace our telephone, computer, television, DVD player, and Internet equipment with one piece of equipment and one provider? What's that one-stop shopping experience going to look like? Ken Kutaragi, CEO of Sony Computer Entertainment, parent company for Sony's mega-product the PlayStation 2, believes that his firm is positioned to take over this process of convergence.

This means that future generations of the PlayStation product will act more and more like a computer with Internet access, a cable television, a DVD player, and a cell phone all rolled into one. Their point of differentiation as a product is that the PlayStation is the most fun computer/DVD/television/telephone on the market. All things being equal, consumer preference may go to more "playful" rather than "professional" products.

PLAY BUSINESS!

Probably the quickest route to jettison any negative baggage from Corporate America is to start playing. Corporate America is all about efficiency. In contrast, play is about waste—wasting time, wasting space, wasting resources. Corporate America is about being serious. Play is about being fun and goofy. Corporate America is about rules but play is about questioning the rules. More creativity happens when people are just "playing around" than when people meet for the "Creativity Summit" in Corporate America.

An attitude of play has been at the heart of almost every technological success story in American business history. Granted, some innovators claim to have created out of either noble or purely financial motives. However, a surprising number use the words "fun" or "toys" when discussing the process of innovation. In his autobiography *My Life and Work*, Henry Ford says of his childhood, "…my mother always said that I was born a mechanic. I had a kind of workshop with odds and ends of metal for tools before I had anything else. In those days we did not have the toys of today; what we had were homemade. My toys were all tools—and they still are! And every fragment of machinery was a treasure."

Not only did Ford view tools as his toys, but consider what he found to be his source of entertainment and education: "Driving to town I always had a

PLAYING WITH TIME

The inventor of our modern system of electronic flash photography just wanted to have some fun. Harold Edgerton began working with strobe lights to study the action of spinning rotors in engines during his graduate studies at the Massachusetts Institute of Technology. In a dark room, the strobe lights could be used to illuminate the mechanics of the engine as it moved at speeds too fast for the human eye to observe. Edgerton had stumbled upon a method of slowing down or stopping high-speed activities so they could be observed more closely.

Not long after, Edgerton started using his knowledge of strobe lights to photograph hundreds of activities never before observed by the human eye. Most of the early experiments were just plain fun. He wondered what a tennis ball looked like as it was being hit off the racket or a baseball as it was hit off the bat. Then he got more complex. Was it possible to photograph a bullet as it popped a balloon? Or as it cut through a card? Or what about an apple? Edgerton succeeded in doing all three and then some.

In his first article for *National Geographic* magazine, Edgerton published a series of photos that stopped the motion of a hummingbird's wings in mid-flight. He also produced an Academy-Award-winning film short. Later, all this fun started to have a broad impact. The military applied several of his discoveries for night surveillance and other clandestine activities. Edgerton developed the camera that photographed the RMS Titanic when it was located in 1986.

pocket full of trinkets—nuts, washers, and odds and ends of machinery. Often I took a broken watch and tried to put it together. When I was thirteen I managed for the first time to put a watch together so that it could keep time. There is an immense amount to be learned simply by tinkering with things. It is not possible to learn from books how everything is made. Machines are to a mechanic what books are to a writer. He gets ideas from them, and if he has any brains he will apply those ideas."

Speaking of Henry Ford, he was a great admirer of Thomas Edison. In fact, before he started the Ford Motor Company he worked as chief engineer at the Edison Illuminating Company's steam generator station in Detroit. Ford admired Edison to such a degree that once Ford became a multimillionaire, he set out to reconstruct pre-industrial America and began purchasing pre-Industrial antiques and artifacts. He assembled this collection in what is now known as Greenfield Village in Dearborn, Michigan. Among the buildings at Greenfield Village you'll find schoolhouses, mills, farmhouses, and even machine shops.

One of the most famous buildings at Greenfield Village is a reconstruction of Edison's Menlo Park laboratory. Ford reconstructed the Wizard's original lab as a gift to honor his famous idol. In fact, so meticulous was the reconstruction that Ford even moved the soil upon which the original lab was built and used it as the foundation to reconstruct the lab in Dearborn. On October 21, 1929 a 50th anniversary celebration of the invention of the incandescent light bulb was held at Greenfield Village (which was then known by its original name of the Edison Institute). Ford invited the now 82-year-old Edison to come to the newly reconstructed Menlo Park lab and reenact the pivotal moment of discovering the filament for the bulb that could burn without consuming itself. Edison gladly accepted the invitation and toured the lab with Ford proudly serving as host. Much to Ford's chagrin, Edison pronounced the recreated laboratory 99.9 percent perfect. When Ford asked his idol what he had missed, Edison responded, "Our floor was never this clean."

Innovation is a messy business. Edison always had more than one thing going in his labs. In 1911, he told an interviewer from *The Century* magazine,

I never think about a thing any longer than I want to. If I lose my interest in it, I turn to something else. I always keep six or eight things going at once, and turn from one to the other as I feel like it. Very often I will work at a thing and get where I can't see anything more in it, and just put it aside and go at something else; and the first thing I know, the very idea I wanted will come to me. Then I drop the other and go back to it and work it out.

Remember, play is against almost everything bureaucracy stands for. Not only is it spontaneous and fun but it takes us in new and unexpected directions and leads us to unexpected, unpredictable outcomes.

E IS FOR EDISON

Key Lesson: Play is to innovation what rules are to bureaucracy.

- Where do you have the most routine in your company? Do you expect your talent to both protect routine and be creative at the same time?
- Where is it possible in your company to allow a more playful culture to grow?
- How can you make what you do more fun for the customer?

Conclusion

GLOW, BUT DON'T
CONSUME YOURSELF

W HEN EDISON DIED IN 1931, HIS MANY ADMIRERS wanted to honor him by shutting off all electric current throughout America for one minute. However, they quickly learned that it was now impossible to stop the flow of electricity in America. The best they could achieve was a general dimming of some of the lights. Within one lifetime, Edison and his electrical inventions had become indispensable. His life and inventions have only continued to increase in importance during the 70 years that have passed since his death.

Edison's lifelong friend and fellow legend Henry Ford said it best when he stated, "To find a man who has not benefited by Thomas Edison and who is not in debt to him, it would be necessary to go deep into the jungle. I hold him to be our greatest American." I agree with Ford. Edison's legacy affects my life from the time I awake to a CD started by my alarm clock to when I turn off the lights at the end of the day. As a matter of fact, each time I answer the telephone, I continue the Edison legacy. One story holds that Edison and his boys made "Hello" the conventional answer when we pick up the telephone. When Alexander Graham Bell and his assistant Thomas Watson were testing their original telephone inventions, they would use the old marine salutation "Ahoy!" as they called back and forth to one another along the wire. When Edison and his boys were developing the carbon transmitter that would make Bell's phone commercially viable, they used "Hello" as they called back and forth to each other at the Menlo Park lab and their greeting became the standard.

The legacy of our greatest American continues to glow seven decades after his passing. Edison's legacy continues because his life exemplified the core principle of the invention most often associated with him—the light bulb. The key to inventing such a bulb was to create a filament that could glow hot enough to produce light but wouldn't destroy itself in the process. Prior to that time, anything that gave off light—like candles or kerosene or the carbon rods in arc-lighting—would consume itself as part of the process. The idea of glowing without consuming yourself is a powerful one. Many people burn very brightly but end up consuming themselves (and often others) along the way. Why do you think we call it "burn-out"? Others, never really catch fire because they never attempt to do anything that will remotely stretch their abilities.

Edison's life story is of a person who glowed but never consumed himself. His life is a record of remarkable accomplishment with patents being filed as late as a few months prior to his death. My challenge to you is to do the same. Like Edison, work hard and stretch yourself with meaningful challenges that leave a legacy that can't be turned off even by those who want to honor you. Also, like Edison, avoid consuming yourself in the process so that you can glow for sixty years or more instead of only ten.

How do you glow without consuming yourself? Here are a few final reminders:

- Choose creativity every day of your life.
- Keep more notes…and do it in the margins.
- When you get really tired, take a break.
- Experiment with everything.
- Have fun…really.
- Give your customers the freedom they deserve.

- Embrace your failures as opportunities for learning.
- Wear looser clothing from time to time.
- Get optimistic about "those crazy kids."
- Take more naps at the office.
- Be nice to the press.
- Get rid of a few of your rules.
- Write more poetry and eat more pie.
- Celebrate your weakness. It's what makes you different.
- Don't worry about capturing every single dollar of value you create.
- Jettison your career and follow your calling.
- Dance around the office when you get a good idea.
- Be excited about your products.
- Be so good they call you a wizard.

I'll let Edison have the last word on this matter, "My philosophy of life is work—bringing out the secrets of nature and applying them for the happiness of man. I know of no better service to render during the short time we are in this world."

ACKNOWLEDGMENTS

I'D LIKE TO THANK THOMAS EDISON FOR ALL THAT HE DID TO make this book possible. First and foremost, I could not have written it without the electricity that makes wordprocessing on a personal computer possible. His invention of the electrical system for homes and offices allowed me to not only write using a personal computer but also light my workspace with electric lights. In addition, Edison is partly responsible for the invention of the computer as we know it today. The vacuum tubes that powered the very first computers were really just modified electric light bulbs.

I would also like to thank Edison for his help in making the copy machine a reality. One of his early inventions evolved into the mimeograph machine that eventually led to the rise of copiers. My library research was made significantly easier as a result of these innovations. I also thank Edison for inventing the recorded music industry. I often listen to music as I write and have found it to be a great stimulus for my creativity.

I am also grateful to Edison for inventing the motion picture industry. Most people know of Edison primarily through two classic films: *Young Thomas Edison* with Mickey Rooney and *Edison, the Man* with Spencer Tracy. These two films have helped the Edison legends continue to grow and expand. In their absence, the audience for this book would be much smaller. Most motion pictures exist on videotape these days and I watched more than my fair share of documentaries about Edison as I researched this book.

I thank Edison for his early innovations on electric storage batteries. I write anywhere and everywhere and often when I'm traveling on airplanes. Without a battery to store electrical power, my laptop computer would just be another heavy piece of carry-on luggage. Also, I'd like to thank Edison for making my university classroom a much more interesting place to teach and learn. The hundreds of students I've had the privilege to teach since becoming a college professor sport some of the most remarkable tattoos in the world. My thanks to Edison for inventing the electric pen that ultimately gave rise to the tattoo industry that thrives in college towns across America.

I would like to acknowledge all of the people working at the Thomas A. Edison Papers Project to make Edison's vast archive of personal papers and experimental records available to the public. The work being done by this project is helping the world understand that Thomas A. Edison was both an inventor and a businessman. In particular, I'd like to thank Bob Rosenberg for helping me answer some key questions during the latter stages of this book. Thanks also to two other scholars associated with this project. First, Andre Millard who was one of the first to dive into the vast Edison archives with the goal of making clear the relationships between Edison's business and technology. His book, *Edison and the Business of Innovation,* forever transformed my appreciation of this great American. Second, thanks to Paul Israel for his incredible biography *Edison: A Life of Invention.* I think each of us—Millard, Israel, and I—are indebted to Thomas P. Hughes whose work, especially *American Genesis,* was among the first to recognize Edison's significant contributions to the American economy. Finally, Tom Standage's outstanding book *The Victorian Internet* helped me confirm my beliefs that Edison and his fellow telegraphers bore more than a passing resemblance to today's computer "nerds."

Thank you to John P. Keegan, Chairman and President of the Charles Edison Fund and the Edison Preservation Foundation for his confirmation that this project was on the right track and his willingness to grace this book with a foreword. I wish him and his staff great success as they work to spread Edison's business story across the globe.

I also wish to acknowledge the true professionals at Entrepreneur Press. My two longsuffering editors on this project, Jere Calmes and Marla Markman, were a constant stream of good counsel. Thank you to Kobina Wright, Kim White, Ron Young, and Neil Perlman at Entrepreneur as well as Beth Hansen-Winter for doing a fabulous design job on the book and Karen Billipp for superb production.

Thanks to Shannon Caraway, P.E., Transmission Support Manager for TXU Electric who was a gracious host and tour guide at the TXU Electric substation in Waco. Also Scott Diermann, Plant Manager for TXU's Lake Creek Plant and Trading House Plant for showing me the basics of electric power generation. I thank my colleagues at Baylor University: Dr. Ben Kelley, Dean of the School of Engineering and Computer Science and Dr. Bill Reichenstein, Professor of Finance, for their helpful comments along the way. Thanks to my graduate assistant Erik Fares for the work he did to help this book keep moving along and to Grant Case for many enjoyable conversations about the current labor market.

Finally, I wish to acknowledge the support and encouragement of my family. Thanks to my parents who are probably my biggest fans. Thanks to my wife, Sarah, who put up with me writing another book after I swore not to write another book for three (or was that five?) years. Thanks also to the two people who make our home the happiest place on earth: Ellis and Miriam.

INDEX